Learning Teaching

A guidebook for English language teachers

Jim Scrivener

MACMILLAN
HEINEMANN
English Language Teaching

Macmillan Heinemann English Language Teaching, Oxford

A division of Macmillan Publishers Limited

Companies and representatives throughout the world

ISBN 0 435 24089 7

Heinemann is a registered trademark of Reed Educational & Professional Publishing Limited

First published 1994

Series design by Mike Brain

Cover photo by Chris Honeywell

Illustrated by Jane Bottomley and Joe Little

The authors and publishers would like to thank the following for
permission to reproduce their material: Cambridge University Press
for the extracts from *New Cambridge English Course* Student's Book 1
(Swan & Walter) on p 39, and from *New Cambridge English Course*
Teacher's Book 1 (Swan & Walter) on pp 40-3; Heinemann ELT for
the extracts from *Flying Colours* Student's Book 2 (Garton-Sprenger &
Greenall) on p 26, *Word Games with English 1* (Howard-Williams &
Herd) on p 84, and *Wordbuilder* (Wellman) on p 85; Longman Group
UK Ltd for the extracts from *The Beginner's Choice* Student's Book 1
(Mohamed & Acklam) on p 158, *The Beginner's Choice* Teacher's
Book 1 (Mohamed & Acklam) on p 58, and *The Sourcebook
Intermediate* (Shepherd, Hopkins & Potter) on p 25; Macmillan ELT
for the extracts from *The Words You Need* (Rudzka, Channell, Putseys
and Ostyn) on pp 91-2; *Time Out* magazine for the advertisement
reproduced in the extract from *The Beginner's Choice* Student's Book 1
on p 158; Adrian Underhill for the phonemic chart on p 141.

Author's acknowledgement
There is a great deal of discussion and exchange of ideas in EFL staff
rooms, corridors, meetings and conferences. I have no idea where I
first came across many of the ideas and suggestions in this book; quite
often I think I've discovered a new technique or activity, only to realize
that it's based on an idea I overheard someone telling someone else a
week before. Thus, my main acknowledgement is to the many teachers
and trainers I have met and been influenced by over the years, and
especially to all those who have worked and argued and discussed and
experimented at IH Hastings.
    There are a number of other strong influences behind this book,
particularly *Freedom to Learn*, by Carl Rogers (Merill 1993), which,
although not specifically about language learning, is a book that made
me rethink my whole attitude to education.
    I first learned about experiential learning cycles from John Heron's
six category invention analysis, currently in print as *Helping the Client*
(Sage 1990).
    Articles by (and discussions with) Adrian Underhill have also
influenced me, particularly Process in Humanistic Education, in
English Language Teaching Journal (ELTJ) 43/4, October 1989. It is one
of Adrian's models that forms the basis for the section in this book on
'Three kinds of teacher'.
    Many thanks also to Vic Richardson for his help.

Printed in Hong Kong

Contents

The Teacher Development Series

TEACHER DEVELOPMENT is the process of becoming the best teacher you can be. It means becoming a student of learning, your own as well as that of others. It represents a widening of the focus of teaching to include not only the subject matter and the teaching methods, but also the people who are working with the subject and using the methods. It means taking a step back to see the larger picture of what goes on in learning, and how the relationship between students and teachers influences learning. It also means attending to small details which can in turn change the bigger picture. Teacher development is a continuous process of transforming human potential into human performance, a process that is never finished.

The Teacher Development Series offers perspectives on learning that embrace topic, method and person as parts of one larger interacting whole. We aim to help you, the teacher, trainer or academic manager to stretch your awareness not only of what you do and how you do it, but also of how you affect your learners and colleagues. This will enable you to extract more from your own experience, both as it happens and in retrospect, and to become more actively involved in your own continuous learning. The books themselves will focus on new treatments of familiar subjects as well as areas that are just emerging as subjects of the future.

The series represents work that is in progress rather than finished or closed. The authors are themselves exploring, and invite you to bring your own experience to the study of these books while at the same time learning from the experiences of others. We encourage you to observe, value and understand your own experience, and to evaluate and integrate relevant external practice and knowledge into your own internal evolving model of effective teaching and learning.

Adrian Underhill

Introduction to *Learning Teaching*

Teacher: One who carries on his education in public (Theodore Roethke)

This book is a guidebook to teaching English as a foreign language. Mostly it is a guide to methodology – to what might work in the classroom.

Learning Teaching is a book that can help you learn to teach in more effective ways. It is also a book about a kind of teaching where the teacher is also learning. However, it is not a book about the right way to teach. Indeed there is no scientific basis yet for writing such a description of an ideal teaching methodology. Instead, we can observe teachers and learners at work and take note of strategies and approaches that seem to be more beneficial than others, not necessarily in order to copy them, but to become more aware of what is possible.

The act of teaching is essentially a constant processing of options. At every point in each lesson a teacher has a number of options available; he or she can decide to do something, or to do something else, or not to do anything at all. In order to become a better teacher it seems important to be aware of as many options as possible. This may enable you to generate your own rules and guidelines as to what works and what doesn't.

Thus, in this book, rather than saying 'This is how to do it,' I've tried to say 'Here are some ways that seem to work.' You'll find lots of ideas and options in these pages and it's largely up to you what you want to take away from them. I aim to give you a 'toolkit' of possibilities.

Who this book is for

This book is designed to help you if any of the following statements are true about you:

- You are doing a training course in English language teaching, such as the RSA/Cambridge Pre-Service or In-Service Certificate in TEFLA, the RSA/Cambridge COTE or the Trinity College Certificate.
- You have moved into English language teaching from teaching other subjects.
- You have started working in a school after an initial training course in English language teaching.
- You are an English language teacher but have had little or no formal training.
- You are an English language teacher and would like a 'refresher course' that looks at current methodology.

In this book I use *he* and *she, him* and *her* largely at random.

About the author

I'm currently working at International House, Hastings where I teach English as a foreign language and work on teacher training courses including the RSA/UCLES Certificate and Diploma (TEFLA), and courses specializing in methodology and the skills of teacher training. I've also taught EFL and trained teachers in Kenya, Georgia, Russia and Malta.

This book is dedicated to Viola and Peter

Chapter 1   Working with people

Introduction

This chapter is an introduction to some of the values and assumptions underlying the methodology in this book. A distinction is drawn between 'teaching' and 'learning' and we start to investigate ways of maximizing learning for both students and teacher.

1   Teaching and learning

Task 1

What does a teacher do? What is your personal image of 'good teaching'? List a number of brief answers.

I'd like to return to these questions and to your own answers later on in this section.

Task 2

Decide what assumptions about the roles of teacher and learners underlie the teaching approach in the classroom picture below.

Fig. 1.1

Commentary ■ ■ ■

For many people this is the conventional image of a schoolroom – the teacher standing at the front of the class 'teaching' and the students sitting in rows listening.

This teaching style is often based on the assumption that the teacher is the 'knower' and has the task of passing over this knowledge to the students. It is sometimes characterized as 'jug and mug' – the knowledge being poured from one receptacle into another empty one. This is probably done mainly by teacher explanations with occasional questions to or from the learners. There seems to be an assumption that having something explained or demonstrated to you will lead to learning. After these explanations, the students will often do some practice exercises to test whether they have understood what they have been told. Throughout the lesson the teacher keeps control of the subject matter, makes decisions about what work is needed and orchestrates what the students do. In this classroom the teacher probably does most of the talking and is by far the most active person.

Many of us are familiar with this kind of situation, having seen it from the student's point of view over many years when we were schoolchildren in school classrooms. We have all been through hundreds of hours of observation of teachers at work and this has probably left a strong image of what teaching is and how it should be done.

In many circumstances teacher lecture or explanation may be an efficient method of informing a large number of people about a topic. However, if our own educational experience has mainly been of this approach then it is worth pausing for a minute and questioning whether this is indeed the most effective or efficient teaching method. Whereas most teachers will need to be good 'explainers' at various points in their lessons, a teaching approach based solely or mainly on this technique can be problematic.

In Fig. 1.1, the teacher is 'teaching', but it is unclear how much 'learning' is taking place. It is tempting to imagine that if one happens then the other must also happen – but in fact 'teaching' and 'learning' need to be clearly distinguished. It is quite possible for a teacher to be putting great effort into his or her teaching and for no learning to be taking place; similarly a teacher could apparently be doing nothing, but the students be learning a great deal.

In the above class of sixteen students one lesson is being 'taught'. But we could equally think of it as sixteen lessons being received.

I'm not involved at all.
I'm tired of sitting on this chair.
I haven't said anything for hours.
Long explanations are so dull – I just turn off.
I didn't understand – and now he's talking about something else.
I'd rather do something different.
He's going too fast.
He's going too slow.
It's not an interesting subject.
I'm not doing anything myself.

Five students are listening and trying to follow the explanations; three others are making detailed notes but not really thinking about the subject; one person is listening and not really understanding anything; one (having missed the previous lesson) thinks that the teacher is talking about something completely different; three students are daydreaming; one is writing a letter; etc.

Here, the teaching is only one factor in what is learned. Indeed teaching is actually rather less important than one might suppose. As a teacher I cannot learn for my students. Only they can do that. What I can do is help create the conditions in which they might be able to learn. This could be by responding to some of the student complaints above – perhaps by involving them, by enabling them to work at their own speed, by not giving long explanations, by encouraging them to participate, talk, interact, do things, etc. ■

Let's look outside the classroom for a moment. How do people learn things in everyday life? Maybe by trial and error. Maybe by reading a DIY manual and following the instructions. Maybe by sitting next to someone who can tell you what to do and give feedback on whether you're doing OK.

The process of learning often involves five steps: (1) doing something; (2) recalling what happened; (3) reflecting on that; (4) drawing conclusions; (5) using those conclusions to inform and prepare for future practical experience. (See Fig. 1.2.)

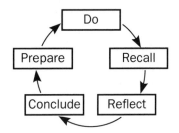

Fig. 1.2: An experiential learning cycle

It is important to distinguish between learning and teaching. Information, guidance and support from other people may come in at any of the five steps of the cycle, as is shown in Fig. 1.3, but the essential learning experience is in doing the thing yourself.

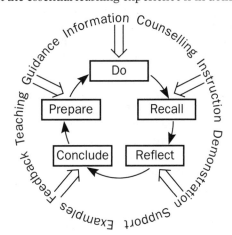

Fig. 1.3: Teaching and the experiential learning cycle

This cycle, known as an *experiential learning cycle*, suggests a number of conclusions for English language teaching in the classroom. For example:

- If this cycle does represent how people learn, then the 'jug and mug' approach may be largely inappropriate if it dominates classroom time. Giving people opportunities to do things themselves may be much more important.
- I may become a better teacher if I worry less about teaching techniques and try to make the enabling of learning my main concern – ie the inner circle of the diagram rather than the outer one.
- I need to ensure that I allow my students practical experience in doing things (eg in *using* language rather than simply listening to lectures *about* language).
- It may be that being 'over-helpful' as a teacher could get in the way of learning. I cannot learn for my students. The more I do myself, the less space there will be for the learners to do things.
- It may be useful to help students become more aware about *how* they are learning, to reflect on this and to explore what procedures, materials, techniques or approaches would help them learn more effectively.
- It's OK for students to make mistakes, to try things out and get things wrong and learn from that.
- ... and that's true for me as a 'learning teacher' as well.

Two assumptions

One fundamental assumption behind this book and the teaching approaches suggested in it is that *people learn more by doing things themselves* rather than by being told about them. This is true both for the students in your classes and for you, as you learn to be a better teacher.

A second assumption is that *learners are intelligent, fully-functioning humans,* not simply receptacles for passed-on knowledge. Learning is not simply a one-dimensional intellectual activity, but involves the whole person.

Recent approaches in EFL have increasingly acknowledged the importance of the 'whole person' in the learner (as opposed to only their mental processes such as thinking, remembering, analyzing, etc). We can no longer be content with the image of the student as a blank slate. Students may bring pen and paper to the lesson. But they also bring a whole range of other, less visible things to class: their needs, their wishes, their life experience, their home background, their memories, their worries, their day so far, their dreams, their anger, their toothache, their fears, their moods, etc. Given the opportunities, they will be able to make important decisions for themselves, to take responsibility for their learning and to move forward (although their previous educational experience may initially predispose them to expecting that you, the teacher, need to do all that for them).

New learning is constructed over the foundations of our own earlier learning. We make use of whatever knowledge and experience we already have in order to help us learn and understand new things. Thus the message taken away from any one lesson is quite different for different people. The new learning has been planted in quite different seed beds. This is true both for your learners meeting a new tense in class and for you reading this paragraph and reviewing it in the light of your own previous experience and knowledge.

Task 3

You are working with this book now – but consider what else is a part of your life at the moment. How many other things are going through your head while you are reading these words? Make a note of a few of these things – previous experiences, knowledge, thoughts, feelings, pains, pleasures, worries, etc. When you've done that, select just one item from your list and consider its involvement with the learning process you are currently going through. Is it helping, or is it distracting you?

The two assumptions listed above inform my teaching. They remind me that my 'performance' as a teacher is only one, possibly minor, factor in the learning that might occur. They remind me that some of the teaching I do might actually prevent learning. They remind me that teaching is, fundamentally, about working with people – and about remaining alive to the many different things that go on when people hack their own path through the jungle towards new learning.

Although this book concentrates mainly on teaching techniques, it is important to bear in mind that knowledge of subject matter and methodology are, on their own, insufficient. A great deal of teaching can be done with those two, but I would suspect that the total learning would not be as great as it could be. However, an aware and sensitive teacher, who respects and listens to her students, and who concentrates on finding ways of enabling learning rather than on performing as a teacher, goes a long way to creating conditions in which a great deal of learning is likely to take place.

Perhaps, then, the first message of this book on methodology is that methodology and knowledge of subject matter are important, but may not necessarily be the most important things.

Task 4

In the classroom pictures below decide what assumptions about the roles of teacher and learners underlie the teaching approaches.

Fig. 1.4

Fig. 1.5

Commentary ■ ■ ■

Compared with the picture at the beginning of this section, it is much harder here to guess which person is the teacher. This may suggest a somewhat different relationship between teacher and students and, possibly, different assumptions about what learning is and how it can be helped. The teacher is no longer the central focus of the class. The activities and the speaking are being done by everyone, rather than only by the person at the front of the room. Without more evidence, it is difficult to draw any definite conclusions, but my initial impression is that in these pictures the learners are not simply receiving passed-on wisdom, but are actively involved in their own learning. It seems possible, therefore, that more learning is actually taking place. ■

Task 5

Look back through the pages you have just been reading. Look back at your own answers to Task 1 on p 1. What was your personal image of a teacher before you started reading? Has that changed at all in response to ideas in the text, or not? How have any new concepts been slotted in with the old? Which ideas have you rejected or postponed consideration of?

2 Three kinds of teacher

This section continues the discussion of different teaching styles begun in the previous section. It starts with a description of three broadly different categories of teacher.

Teacher A: the explainer

Many teachers know their subject matter very well, but have limited knowledge of teaching methodology. This kind of teacher relies mainly on 'explaining' or 'lecturing' as a way of conveying information to the students. Done with style or enthusiasm or wit or imagination this teacher's lessons can be very entertaining, interesting and informative. The students are listening, perhaps occasionally answering questions and perhaps making notes, but are mostly not being personally involved or challenged. The learners often get practice by doing individual exercises after one phase of the lecture has finished.

Teacher B: the involver

This teacher also knows the subject matter that is being dealt with. (In our case this is essentially the English language and how it works.) However, she is also familiar with teaching methodology; she is able to use appropriate teaching and organizational procedures and techniques to help her students learn about the subject matter. 'Teacher explanations' may be one of these techniques, but in her case it is only one option among many that she has at her disposal. This teacher is trying to involve the students actively and puts a great deal of effort into finding appropriate and interesting activities that will do this, while still retaining clear control over the classroom and what happens in it.

Teacher C: the enabler

Essentially teaching is about working with other human beings. This teacher knows about the subject matter and about methodology, but also has an awareness of how individuals and groups are thinking and feeling within her class. She actively responds to this in her planning and working methods and in building effective working relationships and a good classroom atmosphere. Her own personality and attitude are an active encouragement to learning.

This kind of teacher is confident enough to share control with the learners, or to hand it over entirely to them. Decisions made in her classroom may often be shared or negotiated. In many cases she takes her lead *from the students*; seeing herself as someone whose job is to create the conditions that enable the students to learn for themselves. Sometimes this will involve her in less traditional 'teaching'; she may become a 'guide' or a 'counsellor' or a 'resource of information when needed'. Sometimes, when the class is working well under its own steam, when a lot of autonomous learning is going on, she may be hardly visible.

	Subject matter	Methodology	People
Explainer	✓		
Involver	✓	✓	
Enabler	✓	✓	✓

Fig. 1.6: Three kinds of teacher

These three descriptions of teachers are, of course, very broadly painted. There is no way to categorize all teaching under three headings; many teachers will find elements of each category that are true for them, or that they move between categories depending on the day and the class and the aims of a lesson. However, this simple categorization may help you to reflect on what kind of teaching you have mostly experienced in your life so far and may also help you to clarify what kind of teacher you see yourself as being now or in the future.

On teacher training courses I have come across many participants whose initial internal image of a teacher is based on the 'explainer' but who are keen to move to becoming an 'involver'. Such a move may be your aim in reading this book – and the book is mainly geared towards giving you information, ideas, options and starting points that may help you reach that goal. Essentially, therefore, this is a book about methodology. Throughout the book I have also tried to keep in mind the important skills, qualities, values and techniques associated with the 'enabling' teacher and to give guidance and information that may influence your role and relationships in the classroom.

Task 1

Write down the names of some people you have been taught by in the past. When you have a list, go through it and decide which of the three descriptions above (explainer, involver, enabler) best suits each one. This may give you some idea about which images of teaching you have been exposed to and influenced by.

Commentary ■ ■ ■

When I think back on my own experiences of being taught, it is the teaching techniques that I remember least. I certainly remember teachers who made subject matter come alive, through their great knowledge and enthusiasm. But the teacher I recall with most pleasure and respect was the one who listened to me, who encouraged me, who respected my own views and decisions. Curiously this teacher who helped me most was the one who actually did least 'teaching' of the subject matter and was, seemingly, technique-free, being basically 'himself' in class. My memories of his lessons are of what I did, rather than what he did, of my learning rather than his teaching.

Teachers and trainers often comment on the importance of 'rapport' between teachers and students. The problem with rapport is that, whereas it clearly is important, it is also notoriously difficult to define or quantify. It often seems to be the magical ingredient that makes a teacher a teacher – or not. I think rapport is to do with the personal atmosphere a teacher creates in the classroom; the difference, say, between a room where people are defensive and anxious or a room where people feel able to be honest and take risks. In the following list I've noted a number of factors in a teacher that might positively affect the learning atmosphere in a classroom.

The effective teacher ...
- *really* listens to his students;
- shows respect;
- gives clear, positive feedback;
- has a good sense of humour;
- is patient;
- knows his subject;
- inspires confidence;
- trusts people;

- empathizes with students' problems;
- is well-organized;
- paces lessons well;
- does not complicate things unnecessarily;
- is enthusiastic and inspires enthusiasm;
- can be authoritative without being distant;
- is honest;
- is approachable.

Carl Rogers, an American psychologist, suggested that there are three core teacher characteristics that help to create an effective learning environment. These are **respect** (a positive and non-judgmental regard for another person), **empathy** (being able to see things from the other person's perspective, as if looking through their eyes) and **authenticity** (being oneself without hiding behind job titles, roles or masks).

When a teacher has these three qualities, the relationships within the classroom are likely to be stronger and deeper and communication between people much more open and honest. The educational climate becomes positive, forward-looking and supportive. The learners are able to work with less fear of taking risks or facing challenges. In doing this they increase their own self-esteem and self-understanding, gradually taking more and more of the responsibility for their own learning themselves rather than assuming that it is someone else's job.

Carl Rogers considered that, out of these three teacher characteristics, authenticity was the most important. To be yourself. Not to play the role of a teacher – but to take the risk of being vulnerable and human and honest. Gaie Houston (1990) has written that 'The foundation of rapport is to learn yourself enough that you know what style you have and when you are being truthful to yourself.'

Rapport is not a skill or a technique that you can mimic. It is not something you do to other people. It is you and your moment-by-moment relationship with other human beings. Similarly, 'respect' or 'empathy' or 'authenticity' are not clothes to put on as you walk into the classroom, not temporary characteristics that you take on for the duration of your lesson. You cannot roleplay 'respect' – or any of the other qualities. On the contrary, they are rooted at the level of your genuine intentions.

In order to improve the quality of our own relationship in the classroom we do not need to learn new techniques; we need to look closely at what we *really* want for our students, how we really feel about them. It is our attitude and intentions rather than our methodology that we may need to work on. ■

Task 2

Write a brief statement outlining your own assessment of yourself as a teacher (or future teacher). Which kind of teacher do you feel you most resemble? Which would you most like to be? Which of the factors that help effective learning do you think are already present in you? Which are not? Which would you like to work on?

Chapter 4 **Activities and lessons**

Introduction

This chapter offers some basic information and ideas about running lessons and activities. As a starting point we look at the mechanics of a single classroom activity. The aim is to start small and then gradually widen the focus. This chapter comes before Chapter 5 on planning because this reflects the way that I myself learned to teach: I found it hard to worry about the 'bigger' questions until I had gained at least some initial confidence in the basic mechanics of running activities and working with students. If you'd rather have an overview first you could begin by reading Chapter 5.

1 Classroom activities

A basic skill in teaching English as a foreign language is to be able to prepare, set up and run a single classroom activity, for example a game or a communication task or a discussion. This section looks at some typical activities, and considers one in detail. There is also guidance on planning similar activities.

Task 1

Here is some material from a student coursebook. Which of the following activities would it be possible to use Fig. 4.1 for?

a a whole-class discussion of ideas and answers;
b individual written homework;
c a dictation;
d students prepare a short dramatic sketch.

A A teenager wants to go to a party that finishes late. His mother wants him to come home by 10 o'clock, but the teenager wants to stay until midnight. How can he persuade his mother?	**B** A father wants his 18-year-old daughter to go on holiday with her parents. She doesn't want to go . . . she would prefer to go and stay with her friend. How can she persuade her father?

Fig. 4.1: From *The Sourcebook Intermediate,* Shepherd, Hopkins and Potter (Longman 1992)

Commentary ■ ■ ■

Each of these activities is possible by using the same material in different ways. For example:

a The class discuss the problems and possible solutions.
b The students write their feelings about the situations at home or perhaps turn them into a story.

c The teacher dictates a situational description to the students and then invites one student to invent and dictate the first line of the dialogue, then another student does line two, and so on.

d Students make up dialogues in pairs and perform them.

>> Aims p 50

Here we have one piece of material but many possible activities. The activity you will choose will depend on what you want your students to learn from it. Most coursebook material will have clear instructions for doing a single activity with specific aims. You may choose to use the material exactly as the printed instructions tell you to or you can devise simple or imaginative variations to suit your class and its needs. ■

Here is a short random list of some other activities often used in EFL classrooms (out of thousands of possible activities):

- learners do a grammar exercise individually then compare answers with each other;
- learners listen to a taped conversation in order to answer some questions;
- learners write a formal letter;
- learners discuss and write some questions in order to make a questionnaire;
- learners read a newspaper article to prepare for a discussion;
- learners play a vocabulary game;
- learners repeat sentences their teacher is saying;
- learners roleplay a shop scene.

Task 2

Add a few more activities to this list.

Task 3

Read this activity from a student coursebook and answer the questions on content and classroom procedures.

---

6 **Write down the names of three important people in your life (outside your family). Now work in pairs. Exchange lists with your partner and ask each other questions.**

Who's . . . ?
How long have you known him/her?
Where did you meet?
What's he/she like? What's special about him/her?
Do you get on well? Why (not)?

Fig. 4.2: From *Flying Colours* Student's Book 2, Garton-Sprenger and Greenall (Heinemann 1991)

a Content. What language will the students be practising when they do this activity? What other purposes (apart from getting students to practise language) might this activity serve?

b Classroom procedures. How can the teacher organize this activity in class? (ie how can she turn the printed coursebook material into a classroom activity?) How will the instructions be given? What preparations does she need to make? Are any special materials or visual aids needed?

Commentary ■ ■ ■

a When doing this activity the learners will get practice in:
- describing people;
- describing their feelings about people;
- asking questions about the past;
- talking about the past;
- using English to talk about something of personal importance.

As well as working on language, the activity involves students in talking and listening to one another on a personal level. This may help to build good relationships within the class and help create a good working atmosphere.

b There are no special materials or visual aids needed. The teacher has a number of options in organizing the activity. For example, the giving of instructions:
- She could simply tell the class to read the coursebook instructions and do the activity.

>> Instructions
p 97
- She could give instructions orally, perhaps separating three steps: (1) giving instructions for students individually to write three names, and, only when the students have completed that, (2) telling them to get in pairs – and only when the pairs have settled down, then (3) explaining what they have to do in their pairs. Separating activities and instructions into different steps is an important technique. At each point the learners know what they need to know without possible confusion from instructions for later parts of the activity.
- She could demonstrate the activity in front of the whole class, working through an example, rather than simply explaining the instructions. By doing this the learners may become clearer about what the activity involves.

The teacher could, of course, expand on or alter any of the coursebook's suggested steps. She could start with an introduction to the activity or she could include a feedback discussion after the students have finished the communication task. Remember – the coursebook is a starting point and resource; it doesn't have to be precisely obeyed step by step. An important part of your lesson is in the working atmosphere and the relationship that you build with your class – and that is unlikely to be particularly close if you simply direct them mechanically to do exercise after exercise.

Even a simple coursebook instruction like *Now work in pairs* offers the teacher options. For example, she could tell each student who he or she must work with (ie *Petra work with Christina*), or the students could choose for themselves, or the pairings could be the result of some random game or humorous instruction (eg *Find someone whose shoes are a different colour from your own*). ■

Task 4

Below is a brief description of a teacher – Riccardo – using the above activity in his class of seventeen young adults. Before you read it, visualize for yourself what might happen. What are the learners doing? What is the atmosphere in the classroom like?

> Riccardo says, *I've been thinking about important people in my life. Not my family – but other people. For example – George. Do you know George?*
> Some of the students say *No.*
> *Ah – you don't know George?* continues Riccardo, putting on a 'mysterious' expression. *Ask me some questions – can you find out some information about George?*

The students have had their curiosity aroused by this very simple withholding of information and now begin to ask questions to find out about this person. When it gets too noisy Riccardo uses gestures to indicate which student should speak next. He also encourages students to rephrase or correct each other when their questions contain errors related to the language aim of the activity. Sometimes he corrects an error himself.

Finally, after eight or nine questions and answers, the identity of George is established as the person who is teaching Riccardo to play the saxophone. A brief conversation about musical likes and dislikes ensues. When that finishes Riccardo asks the students to think back to the questions they had asked him. As they recall questions (eg *When did you meet him?*) Riccardo writes them up on the board.

When a number of questions are up, Riccardo says *OK – now it's your turn to play the game. Write down three names of people who are important in your life. Don't write any information – just their names. And choose people that no one else here knows. So – for example – don't put my name – because you all know me!*

He waits while the students do this, keeping an eye out for the moment when the majority of them have finished. Then he says *We're going to work in pairs – find someone to work with.* Chaos follows for a minute or so while students reorganize themselves. Some walk across the room to find a partner, some just turn to the person next to them.

When they are sitting down again, he says *Show your partner one of the names you have written. Your partner must ask questions to find out information about the person. You can use the questions on the board to help you.* The students start talking in pairs. There is a lot of noise from the conversations. Riccardo wanders around the room at the start of the activity to check that the students have understood the instructions and are doing what was asked. He then sits quietly in a corner of the room apparently taking little notice of what the students are doing. At one point a student asks Riccardo for help – a word he can't remember – but Riccardo politely refuses to help. The conversations continue for about seven minutes.

When most have finished talking, Riccardo calls attention back to himself by standing up and saying *OK,* and waiting for silence. Then he asks *Did you find out about any interesting people?* A short feedback discussion starts. One student says *Mario has a friend who fishes sharks...*

Task 5

Look back at the description of the activity. Which of the following sentences are true?

a The teacher demonstrated how to do the activity rather than simply giving instructions.

b The teacher clearly separated the various steps of the planned activity.

c The teacher corrected the students in some parts of the activity but not in others.

d The teacher made sure that the students had some idea about the language they could use before he asked them to do the activity.

e The teacher had thought of one possible problem with the activity and therefore tried to prevent this by giving an additional instruction.

Commentary ■ ■ ■

a True. Riccardo started by telling the class George's name and encouraging them to question him – precisely what the students would soon do themselves.

b True.

c True. He corrected (and encouraged student correction) at the beginning when the class was working with him – but when the pairwork started he did no correction at all.

》 Errors and correction p 109

d True. He gave the students the chance to hear and use the language during his 'George' example – and some of these sentences were later written up on the board for students to refer to if they needed to.

e True. Riccardo had thought that the activity would probably work less well if they chose people their partner already knew (there would be less need for questions and answers). ■

Task 6

What is your opinion about the following things that happened during the activity – do you think they were appropriate or useful? Would you do the same or not?

a Some of the activity involved the whole class working together. Some of the activity involved students working in pairs.

b There were a number of very noisy stages in the activity – eg when the students were changing places, and when they were all talking to each other.

c Riccardo allowed a brief diversion from his plan while they talked about music.

d Riccardo refused to help a student who wanted his help.

Commentary ■ ■ ■

a There are four typical arrangements common in English language teaching classrooms: whole class; small groups; pairs; and individual work. It is often useful to include a variety of groupings in a lesson.

《 Classroom interaction p 13

b Learning is often quite a noisy business. If people speak or move or do things then there is very likely to be noise – especially if lots of people are doing things at the same time. Obviously sometimes noise serves no useful purpose – but it is often evidence that a lot of important work is going on.

c This diversion allowed students to talk about something of interest to them without deviating from the original lesson plan for too long. I usually feel that such moments are not wasted time but are actually very important. For once the students are using English to do something *they* want to do – rather than something I have asked them to do!

d At first glance this seems rather cruel. Is it possible that it is sometimes more useful for a teacher *not* to help than to help? ■

The following plan describes one possible route-map for running a simple activity:

Before the lesson

1 Familiarize yourself with the material and the activity. Try the activity yourself. Imagine how it will look in class. Decide how many organizational steps are involved. How long will it probably take? Do the learners know enough language to be able to make a useful attempt at the activity? What help might they need? What questions might they have? What errors are they likely to make? What will the teacher's role be at each stage? What instructions are needed? How will they be given? (Explained? Read? Demonstrated?) Prepare any aids or additional material.

You also need to think through any potential problems or hiccups in the procedures. For example, what will happen if you plan student work in pairs but there is an uneven number of students? Will this student work alone or will you join in or will you make one of the pairs into a group of three?

In the lesson

2 Pre-activity: introduction and lead-in to activity. This may be to help raise motivation or interest (eg discussion of a picture related to the topic), or perhaps to focus on language items (eg items of vocabulary) that might be useful in the activity.

3 Set up the activity (or if it is complex, set up the first step of the activity). Organize the students so that they can do the activity. (This may involve making pairs or groups, moving the seating, etc). Give clear instructions for the activity. A demonstration or example is usually much more effective than a long explanation. You may wish to check back that the instructions have been understood (eg *So, Georgi, what are you going to do first?*). In some activities it may be useful to allow some individual work (eg thinking through a problem, listing answers, etc) before the students get together with others.

4 Run the activity (or the first step). If the material was well-prepared and the instructions clear, then the activity can now largely run itself. Allow the students to work on the task without too much interference. The teacher's role now is much more low-key, taking a back seat and monitoring what is happening without getting in the way. Beware of encumbering the students with unnecessary help. This is their chance to work. If it's difficult, give them the chance to rise to that challenge, without leaning on you.

5 Close the activity (or the first step). Allow it to close properly. Rather than suddenly stopping the activity at a random point, try to sense when the students are ready to move on. If different groups are finishing at different times, make a judgement about when coming together as a whole class would be useful to most people. If you want to close the activity while many students are still working, give a time warning (eg *Finish the item you are working on* or *Two minutes*).

6 If the activity is complex and involves more than one step, repeat points 3, 4 and 5 for subsequent steps.

7 Post-activity. It may be useful to have some kind of feedback session on the activity. This could involve comparing opinions from different groups, checking answers, looking at problems arising, discussing the purpose of the activity and reactions to it, continuing interesting discussions, etc. It can be rather dull simply to go over things that have already been done thoroughly in small groups. Aim to get as many students as possible involved in speaking and participating. For example, when checking answers it may be more interesting for groups to exchange and compare their answers themselves, than for the teacher to be up at the front asking for and checking them.

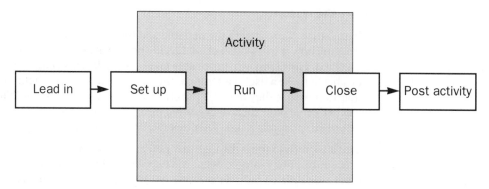

Fig. 4.3: Procedure for running an activity

Task 7

Here is an excerpt from a student coursebook aimed at beginners (the students may know some English but are very limited in knowledge of vocabulary, grammar, etc). The instructions for activities 1–4 have been removed. Write in appropriate instructions for each activity.

Fig. 4.4: From *The Beginner's Choice* Student's Book 1, Mohamed and Acklam (Longman 1992)

Commentary ■ ■ ■

The original instructions were:

1 Match the words to the picture above.
2 Ask and answer with another student.
3 Use the ideas below to give advice, using *should/shouldn't*.
4 Have a complete conversation with another student.

Your instructions may have been different, but possibly equally appropriate. Any one piece of material could be used in a variety of ways. ■

Task 8

Choose one of the four activities you looked at in Task 7. Plan a basic procedure for using it in class, using the seven steps described on pp 29–30.

In your early lessons as an English teacher you may find that 'survival' is your main priority. You would like to teach well and for your students to learn and enjoy what happens, but above even that you want something that you can prepare easily, something that is guaranteed (or nearly guaranteed) to work; something that will let you go into the classroom, do some useful work with the learners and get out alive.

If you have a coursebook then you have an instant source of material. Many teachers also use ideas books, known as 'recipe books', which do exactly what that nickname suggests – give you everything you need to know to be able to walk into class with the right ingredients to 'cook up' a good activity.

As a starting point, a 'survival lesson' could be simply a series of activities following on from each other, one after the other. For one or two lessons this is probably workable. Clearly, though, it is soon going to be unsatisfactory as the basis of a whole course: where is the direction, the growth, the progress? What about the students' needs, their personalities, their likes? Activities such as we have been looking at are the building blocks, but we now need to consider much more carefully how we connect them together.

2   Four kinds of lesson

A complete lesson may consist of a single long activity, or it may have a number of shorter activities within it. These activities may have different aims; they may also, when viewed together, give the entire lesson an overall objective. This section of the book looks at some ways in which activities can relate to each other and combine to make a complete lesson.

Here is a description of four basic lesson types:

1   Logical line

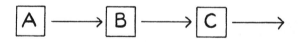

In this lesson there is a clear attempt to follow a 'logical' path from one activity to the next. Activity A leads to activity B leads to activity C. Activity C builds on what has been done in activity B, which itself builds on what has been done in activity A.

In work on grammar, for example, the sequence of activities might be: A – first we understand an item of language; B – we practice it orally in drills; C – we get practice using it in more unrestricted, integrated speaking work; D – we do some written exercises to consolidate our understanding.

In work on language skills, the sequence of activities often moves from an overview towards work on specific details. For example, the learners move gradually from a general understanding of a reading text to detailed comprehension and study of items within it.

There is probably one clear overall objective to the whole lesson. The teacher has predicted possible problems and difficulties and has prepared ways to deal with them when they come up in class.

The teacher is hoping to lead the learners step by step through a clearly programmed sequence of activities in the hope of them all reaching a specific, pre-determined end point. I imagine the class going down a long, straight road, led by the teacher, who takes care that any stragglers catch up and that any wanderers find the right path again.

Many teacher training courses encourage you to prepare lessons of this kind. This is partly because it is possible for trainers and trainees to sort out a lot of potential problems at the planning stage and partly because the lessons are easier for an observer to evaluate, though there is no particular evidence to suggest that this type of lesson is any more successful than others in enabling effective learning.

The following description of a 'logical line' lesson is subdivided into four distinct stages, four separate activities, but it is also clear that it all adds up to a total lesson.

1 The teacher asks the students which makes of cars they have heard of. Which ones do they like? Which don't they like? Why?
2 The teacher says some comparative sentences about cars. For example: *A Porsche is faster than a Mini. A Mini is cheaper than a Rolls-Royce,* etc. The students get a number of opportunities to repeat the teacher's sentences and to make some new ones of their own.
3 Students are given a number of car advertisements and a blank grid to fill out using information from the ads: price, maximum speed, etc. The students work in pairs to find the answers.
4 Students then use this information to discuss which car they would like to have and giving reasons (ie using comparatives). The teacher encourages and helps them to use comparative sentences accurately.

Task 1

Make a simple plan (similar to the description above) for a 'logical line' lesson where the aim is to practise writing the past simple tense using a picture story.

2 Topic umbrella

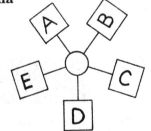

In this kind of lesson, a topic (eg *rain forests* or *education* or *weather* or *good management*) provides the main focal point for student work. The teacher might include a variety of separate activities (eg on vocabulary, speaking, listening, grammar, etc) linked only by the fact that the umbrella topic remains the same.

The activities can often be done in a variety of orders without changing the overall success of the lesson. In some cases activities may be linked; for example, when the discussion in one activity uses vocabulary studied in a preceding activity.

There may be a number of related or disparate aims in this lesson, rather than a single main objective.

Task 2

Here is a description of a 'topic umbrella' lesson for an elementary level class. The activities are not given in their original order.

1 Mark each activity with the main language system or skill focused on (eg listening).
2 In what order do you think the activities were done?

a Learners in pairs read a newspaper advertisement for a sports centre and find out what time they must go and how much it will cost.
b The teacher hands out a list of sports. In pairs the learners choose a sport they would like to do together that evening.
c The teacher asks the learners if they have ever been to a sports centre. What is inside? What are the advantages of a sports centre? Disadvantages? They discuss the topic for a few minutes.
d The teacher explains that they will hear a radio advertisement for a sports centre. They must listen and find out whether their sport is available.
e The teacher asks the learners to make sentences about sports using the construction *I like X but I prefer Y* and *I can't stand Z* (eg *I like squash but I prefer table tennis, I can't stand football*). The learners get some oral practice (with correction) in saying these sentences accurately and with good pronunciation.

Commentary ■ ■ ■

Language area focused on: **a** – reading; **b** – speaking; **c** – speaking; **d** – listening; **e** – grammar.

Either **b** or **c** would make a good introduction to the lesson, introducing the topic of sport and sports centres. Activity **d** (followed by **a**) must come *after* the pairs have chosen their sport; there would be no point in doing **d** after **a** as the answer would be known already. The language work in **e** could come at any point; a suitable place seems to be after the vocabulary in **b** has been introduced and before the listening and reading work. Thus, a likely order would be **c b e d a** or **b c e d a**. It would be possible to put the discussion at the end of the lesson: **b e d a c** (though it seems better value to use the discussion at the beginning as a way into the topic). ■

3 Jungle path

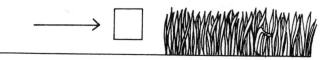

The 'logical line' and 'topic umbrella' lessons both involve the teacher pre-planning a sequence of activities; the teacher usually feels able to predict what language areas will be worked on, what problems are likely to arise and what the students are likely to achieve in the lesson.

An alternative approach would be *not* to predict and prepare so much but to create the lesson moment by moment in class, the teacher and learners working with whatever is happening in the room, responding to questions, problems and options as they come up and finding new activities, materials and tasks in response to particular situations. The starting point might be an activity or a piece of material, but what comes out of it will remain unknown until it happens. The essential difference between this lesson and the previous lesson types is that the teacher is working more with the people in the room than with her material or her plan.

I imagine a group of people hacking their way through the jungle towards new experiences, new learnings. Sometimes the teacher may lead, sometimes the students. Everyone would be encouraged to think, make connections, ask questions and draw conclusions for themselves.

The main pre-planning for a lesson of this kind would involve the teacher using her knowledge of the learners and of the available resources to choose some activities and materials that are likely to prove challenging and raise important questions and issues. She would have an intuitive sense of various potential links between activities, based partly on previous experiences of the outcomes of lessons using similar activities.

In class some of these activities and materials may be used, some not. The teacher may also feel the need to find other materials as the lesson proceeds, some from a coursebook, some from her head, some from her staffroom library, etc. Although she may be clear about a number of possible directions the lesson might take, it will be impossible for her to state the lesson's objectives until after it has finished.

Here is an example lesson description:

Lesson a

1 The teacher takes a communication game (concerning different attitudes to smoking) into class. The students do this in pairs.
2 When they have finished, some students ask about a number of language problems they had. The students discuss and work out some answers to the problems.
3 The teacher invents a quick practice exercise that will focus on one of the language points.
4 When that has finished, a student asks about the pronunciation of some words in the exercise. The teacher works through some examples on the board and then tells them to turn to a page in their coursebook where there is a game to help raise students' awareness of word stress. The class decides that they don't want to do this now, but will do it for homework.
5 Some students remind the teacher that they haven't yet discussed smoking as a whole class and they'd like to hear what some of the rest of the class thought ... etc.

Here are two common examples of a 'jungle path' lesson where the teacher starts without any materials:

Lesson b

The teacher asks *How was the weekend?* (or a similar question), and after listening to a number of answers, leads this into a discussion based on something a student said. At some point she selects particular items of language that a student has used, focuses on these (perhaps considering grammar or pronunciation), invents a simple exercise that will help students work on this, etc etc.

Lesson c

A student asks a question at the start of the lesson. This leads into some work on the board (perhaps the teacher sets the class a problem to solve that will help to clarify the language difficulty). While the students are working on the puzzle, the teacher goes to the staffroom and collects a further exercise on the same language area. He returns and offers the students the new exercise, but they say they feel clear now about the language item. However, there is another question which has arisen ...

A fourth example lesson demonstrates how a competent and confident teacher might hand over responsibility and decision making entirely to the class:

Lesson d

The teacher starts the lesson by asking *What shall we work on today?* She then waits while the class decides, taking care not to manipulate them into deciding something that she wants them to do. Once the decisions are made, she does whatever she has been asked to do.

The 'jungle path' lesson can look artless to an observer, yet to do it successfully requires experience. It is not simply a 'chat' or an abdication of responsibility, though in inexperienced hands it might well be simply a muddle and a 'lazy' alternative to careful planning. In fact, a competent teacher is working minute by minute with her class, actively planning and re-planning as she goes, constantly basing the work around the students and their needs, statements, problems, questions, etc.

A teacher doing this needs to be aware both of the people in the room and of the wide variety of options open to her. She needs to be able to make decisions, moment by moment, about which route is the best one to follow. She needs to be familiar with all the resources of material and information available to her.

The need for teaching experience and awareness of resources available suggests that lessons of this type are more appropriate for teachers who are already fairly competent in planning and executing lessons of the 'logical line' or 'topic umbrella' variety. For this reason it is the lesson you don't normally learn to do on teacher-training courses!

4 Rag-bag

This lesson is made up of a number of unconnected activities. For example: a chat at the start of the lesson, followed by a vocabulary game, a pairwork speaking activity and a song. The variety in a lesson of this kind may often be appealing to students and teacher. There can, however, be a 'bittiness' about this approach that makes it unsatisfactory for long-term usage.

There will be no overall language objective for the lesson (though there might be a 'group-building' aim). Each separate activity might have its own aims.

LESSON TYPE	NATURE OF LINK BETWEEN ACTIVITIES	SOME OUTCOMES OF EFFECTIVE USE	SOME OUTCOMES OF INEPT OR LAZY USE
Logical line	Straight line	Clearly visible progress	Limited response to individual needs
	Programmed growth	Focuses towards an aim	Atomistic; hard to see the overview
Topic umbrella	Topic	Variety	Tenuous links to boring topics
		Framework for learning	Easily becomes rag-bag
Jungle path	Evolutionary	Person-centred	Muddled
		Responsive to immediate needs	Aimless
		Powerful personal insights	An escape from planning and preparation
			Easily becomes rag-bag
Rag-bag	None	Variety	Going nowhere
		Surprise	Students wait for teacher's next surprise
		Entertainment	

Fig. 4.5: Four types of lesson

Task 3

Of the four lesson types, which do you feel most comfortable with? Which ones have you not tried? Which would you be interested to try?

Task 4

Is there a fifth lesson type that you use or are aware of?

3   Using a coursebook

This section looks in detail at one unit from a coursebook in order to analyze what it includes and to consider how such material might be used in class.

A coursebook can be a good source of useful, exploitable material. It will also sequence the activities. Sadly, not all coursebooks are equally helpful, but as a starting point I'd certainly recommend finding out if your book is usable or not. (At the very least your students will probably expect you to use the book and starting with what they expect is probably quite sensible.)

Of course, you do not necessarily need to be a slave to the book; you can adapt and vary the activities if you wish; you can do them in a different order; you can omit some of them or all of them.

Similarly, you can, if you wish, do precisely what the book suggests you do. In your early days of teaching, doing precisely what the book suggests can be a very good way of learning how to teach.

The coursebook writer is a more experienced teacher than you and knows something of the problems learners have, provides a useful syllabus for them to follow, and has devised a course to help them learn. The questions in Task 1 below are intended to make you more aware of the aims of coursebook material and to start you thinking about ways to exploit that material in class.

Task 1

Look at the page from the *New Cambridge English Course 1* (Fig. 4.6), a widely used course aimed at beginners and low level classes of learners.

Study the page, doing the questions below (continued on p 40) in turn. You'll find answers and commentary following the task.

1   What are the main areas of grammar, function, vocabulary or phonology that the lesson is working on?
2   This question is about what the *learners* might do in this lesson. Assume that the exercises are done in the ways suggested by the book's instructions. Mark letters beside the seven activities as follows: **S** (a lot of speaking); **L** (a lot of listening); **R** (a lot of reading); **W** (a lot of writing); **T** (a lot of thinking). Note: an exercise may not clearly indicate how it can be done (the teacher or students could therefore choose how to do it). A single exercise might also involve more than one of these categories.
3   Which activities would you categorize as 'games' or 'game-like'?
4   Although the activities may look straightforward to us, they could prove very challenging to the learners. What do you think will challenge them in each activity?
5   Which activities relate the language to true personal information about the learners?
6   Visualize yourself as the teacher using this lesson. Where are you standing or sitting at each point in the lesson? How much are you talking? What are you saying? What are you doing? Divide the activities into 'teacher does a lot'; 'teacher does some things' and 'teacher does very little'.
7   What would your classroom procedure be for using the material in Exercise 1? (ie what activity would you organize to exploit the material?)
8   If the learners do not know what *bored* means, at what stage of the lesson do you think they will learn it?
9   *How* will they learn it? From what or from whom will they learn it?

Unit 10 Wanting things

10A I'm hungry

Feelings; places; *be* and *have*; sentences with *when*.

1 Put the adjectives with the right pictures. Use your dictionary.

hungry   tired   ill   happy   cold   dirty   bored   unhappy   thirsty   hot

1. She is ....   2. He is ....   3. She is ....   4. He is ....   5. She is ....

6. He is ....   7. She is ....   8. He is ....   9. She is ....   10. She is ....

2 Say how you feel now. Examples:

'I'm very hungry.'
'I'm quite tired.'
'I'm a bit cold.'
'I'm not very happy.'
'I'm not at all thirsty.'

3 Mime one of the adjectives for the class.

4 Say these words and expressions.

hungry   happy   unhappy
house   home   at home
hotel   Hilton Hotel   holiday
on holiday   hair   have   half
hundred   a hundred   him
her

5 Have you got a good memory? Look at the sentences for two minutes. Then close your book and answer the teacher's questions.

When Fred's hungry he goes to a restaurant.
When Lucy's hungry she has bread and cheese.
When Fred's thirsty he has a beer.
When Lucy's thirsty she has a drink of water.
When Fred's bored he goes to the cinema.
When Lucy's bored she goes to see friends.
When Fred's hot he goes to the swimming pool.
When Lucy's hot she has a drink of water.
When Fred's dirty he has a bath.
When Lucy's dirty she has a shower.
When Fred's happy he goes shopping.
When Lucy's happy she telephones all her friends.
When Fred's unhappy he goes to bed.
When Lucy's unhappy she goes shopping.
When Fred's ill he goes to the doctor.
When Lucy's ill she goes to bed.

6 What do you do when you're happy, unhappy, tired, bored, etc.?

7 You're in one of these places. Do a mime; the class will say where you are.

at a swimming pool   at a disco   at a restaurant
in bed   in the bathroom   at a car park
at the doctor's   at the dentist's   at a supermarket
at a clothes shop   at home   at school
at a bus stop   at a station   at a hotel

Learn: water; hungry; thirsty; hot; cold; happy; unhappy; bored; tired; ill; dirty; not at all (*with adjectives*); when (*conjunction*); (have a) bath; (have a) shower; go shopping.

Learn some of these if you want: restaurant; hotel; cinema.

Fig. 4.6: From *New Cambridge English Course* Student's Book 1, Swan and Walter (CUP 1990)

10 What are the language aims of Exercise 5? What do you think the 'teacher's questions' will be?

11 If you were working with this page in class, are there any parts you might omit (because they are complicated, boring, confusing; because you just don't like them, etc)? Which parts might you need to plan carefully if you had a particularly shy or self-conscious class?

12 Why might you want to add something of your own (or from another source)? Think of one activity (perhaps very short) to supplement what is on this page.

Commentary ■ ■ ■

1 The main grammatical and functional areas are summarized in the top right-hand corner of the students' page. A list of vocabulary is in the bottom right-hand corner. Look also at these notes from the teacher's book:

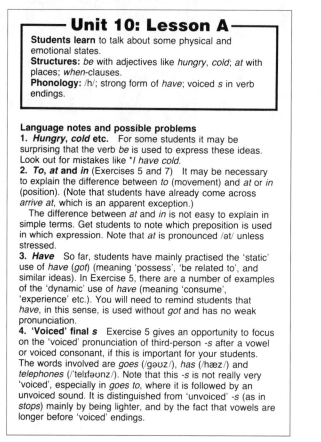

┌─── **Unit 10: Lesson A** ───┐

Students learn to talk about some physical and emotional states.
Structures: *be* with adjectives like *hungry, cold*; *at* with places; *when*-clauses.
Phonology: /h/; strong form of *have*; voiced *s* in verb endings.

Language notes and possible problems
1. *Hungry, cold* etc. For some students it may be surprising that the verb *be* is used to express these ideas. Look out for mistakes like **I have cold.*
2. *To, at* and *in* (Exercises 5 and 7) It may be necessary to explain the difference between *to* (movement) and *at* or *in* (position). (Note that students have already come across *arrive at*, which is an apparent exception.)
 The difference between *at* and *in* is not easy to explain in simple terms. Get students to note which preposition is used in which expression. Note that *at* is pronounced /ət/ unless stressed.
3. *Have* So far, students have mainly practised the 'static' use of *have* (*got*) (meaning 'possess', 'be related to', and similar ideas). In Exercise 5, there are a number of examples of the 'dynamic' use of *have* (meaning 'consume', 'experience' etc.). You will need to remind students that *have*, in this sense, is used without *got* and has no weak pronunciation.
4. 'Voiced' final *s* Exercise 5 gives an opportunity to focus on the 'voiced' pronunciation of third-person *-s* after a vowel or voiced consonant, if this is important for your students. The words involved are *goes* (/gəʊz/), *has* (/hæz/) and *telephones* (/'telɪfəʊnz/). Note that this *-s* is not really very 'voiced', especially in *goes to*, where it is followed by an unvoiced sound. It is distinguished from 'unvoiced' *-s* (as in *stops*) mainly by being lighter, and by the fact that vowels are longer before 'voiced' endings.

2 1 RTW;   2 STL;   3 ST;   4 SLT;   5 TLS or W;   6 STL;   7 ST

3 Activities 1, 3, 5 and 7 all seem to have 'game-like' features in them. (1: matching pictures and words; 3: miming and guessing; 5: memory game; 7: mime and guessing)

4 1: Matching words to pictures; finding words in dictionary; understanding new words; learning new words.
2: Manipulating sentences; pronouncing accurately; finding the right language to say something true about themselves.
3: Miming accurately; guessing mimes; finding the right language to make a guess;

Pairs interview

❯❯ Icebreakers
p 164

This is useful at the start of a course to help people get to know one another and to create a friendly working relationship. It also establishes the fact that speaking is an important part of a course right from the start.

Put the students into pairs. They should interview the other students, asking any question they wish, and noting down interesting answers. When finished they introduce the person they interviewed to the rest of the class (or to a small group of students).

If you are concerned that the class may not have enough language to be able to ask questions, you could start the activity by eliciting a number of possible questions from the students.

Pairs compare

This activity goes a little deeper than the one before. It's useful at the start of a course, but also at other points, to allow people to find out more about one another.

First stage: filling the grid dictation
Give one copy of the grid below to each student. Give instructions for words or pictures to be put in each square. For example: *Write the name of your favourite film in box 7; Draw your favourite food in box 2; Write your favourite English word in box 12; What is your dream? Draw it in box 6; What are you worried about at the moment? Put that in box 9; etc.*
You can vary the instructions depending on the age, experience, English level, etc of the class. Once they've got the idea encourage them to offer instructions, too. Go on until the grid is filled.

Second stage: comparison, discussion
In pairs (or small groups) the students can now compare what they have put in the grid. Many small discussion topics can easily grow out of this.

Third stage: whole class
After sufficient time for a good conversation in the pairs or groups, you may want to draw together any particularly interesting ideas or comments with the whole class.

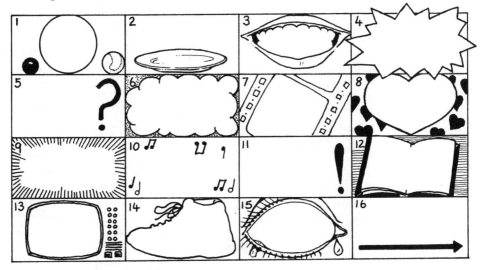

Fig. 6.2: Pairs compare grid

Picture difference

In pairs, one student is given picture A, one picture B. Without looking at the other picture they have to find the differences (ie by describing the pictures to each other).

Fig. 6.3: Picture difference

Stamp collecting

Divide the class into groups of four students. Tell them that they are stamp collectors and that they desperately want three more stamps to finish their collection. They also have a number of stamps available to give away or swap. The students sit apart from each other so that they cannot see what stamps the others have got.

Photocopy groups of stamps such as the ones below a number of times. Cut the sheets up and make 'wants' cards – each with three stamps on. Hand these out and also randomly distribute a number of individual 'stamps'. The students must 'telephone' each other and describe the stamps they want, trying to find out if another student has them. They do not look at each other's collection! If they think they have found a stamp they want then they make an agreement to exchange but *still do not look or exchange*. At the end of the game, when all bargains have been made, the students can then meet up and pass over the agreed stamps and see if they have got what they wanted or not!

Fig. 6.4: Stamp collecting

Planning a holiday

Collect together a number of advertisements or brochures advertising a holiday. Explain to the students that we can all go on holiday together, but we must all agree on where we want to go. Divide the students into groups of three and give each group a selection of this material. Their task is to plan a holiday for the whole group (within a fixed budget per person). Allow them a good amount of time to read and select a holiday and then to prepare a presentation in which they attempt to persuade the rest of the class that they should choose this holiday. When they are ready, each group makes their presentation and the class discusses and chooses a holiday.

Survival

Tell a *lost in the forest* story. Make it dramatic (invent the details). Include a disaster of some kind, eg minibus crashes miles from anywhere, injuries, etc. Give them the map and the notes. Students must plan what they should do to have the best chance of survival.

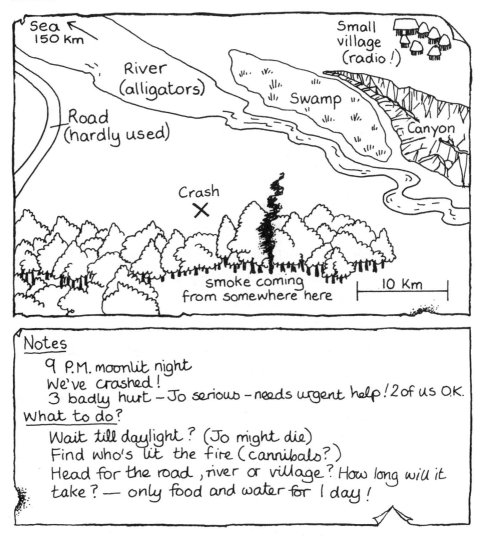

Fig. 6.5: Survival

Whole class puzzle

Here is a fascinating whole class exercise. This is a remarkably simple exercise that really gets groups working together especially if you, the teacher, offer minimal or no help. If you want to be really bold, give no instructions at all! Otherwise you may wish to explain that you have written some sentences about a common object – for example, a pen or a guitar, but every time the name of the object appears you have written *splurg* instead. The task is, of course, to find out what a *splurg* is.

Photocopy and cut up the *splurg* sentences (Fig. 6.6, including the two introductory ones). Hand out one or more to each student (so that they are all given out) and leave them to it. You don't need to help them or speak to them until they have agreed on an answer. If you find that you do wish to help them you could offer information on which sentences are true and which untrue.

If you can't do the puzzle yourself, you'll find the answer on p 72.

What are *splurgs*?

Some of these sentences are untrue:

There are special *splurgs* to use in the car.

Splurgs are usually made mainly of plastic and metal.

You can often find something made of paper inside them.

Splurgs need electricity to work.

Babies are sometimes frightened by *splurgs*.

Splurgs make a noise when you use them.

People throw away what they find inside *splurgs*.

Splurgs usually have long wires.

Splurgs are often used in this school, but not by the students or teachers.

Splurgs feature in a famous spy novel.

Splurgs help to keep a place clean.

You can buy *splurgs* at a newsagent's.

You need at least a day's training before you can use a *splurg*.

Most *splurgs* are about five centimetres long.

Most *splurgs* are red, a few are orange or pink, and there is one famous one in the USA that is green.

Splurgs are mainly used by men.

Fig. 6.6: *Splurgs*

3 Fluency and communication

Here are some things you will probably hear people say – students, other teachers and maybe even yourself.

*But I don't want to talk to other students. They speak badly. I just want to listen to **you** speak.*

I speak a lot but what is the point if you never correct me? I will never improve.

You should be teaching them – not just letting them chatter away. That's lazy teaching.

I don't need to speak. Teach me more grammar. I will speak later.

There's no point doing this task if we use bad English to do it.

This is just a game. I paid a lot of money and now I have to play a game.

Task 1

Take sides. Rehearse your arguments and replies to some or all of the above.

Commentary ■ ■ ■

I didn't have a tape recorder with me but I've often overheard this conversation:

STUDENT: *I speak a lot but what is the point if you never correct me? I will never improve.*
TEACHER: *I don't think it's true that I never correct you. Do you remember the first lesson this morning when we were studying the conditional sentences? There was a lot of correction then. Also in the speaking exercise you are talking about now, we spent ten minutes after it finished looking at some problems.*
STUDENT: *But when I am speaking I make mistakes all the time. That is when you must say me that I am wrong.*
TEACHER: *What would happen to the activity if I stopped people all the time and told them about their mistakes? Would you still be able to speak?*
STUDENT: *Well, I am not agree ...*
TEACHER: *Disagree.*
STUDENT: *I disagree because I want speak.*
TEACHER: *to.*
STUDENT: *I want to speak.*
TEACHER: *Listen to the pronunciation: /tə spiːk/.*
STUDENT: *You are correcting me all the time to show me that it is not good?*
TEACHER: *Yes. When you speak you need to work on two things. One is accuracy – getting everything correct. But the other is fluency – speaking at a good speed and communicating easily with other people. It's very important to practise that as well as working on reducing mistakes. So in some activities I focus on accuracy but in others I focus on fluency, and if I want to do any work on the language you use I wait until after you have finished, so that I don't interrupt you and interfere with your speaking. If I corrected while you were speaking there would be less communication.*
STUDENT: *But there's no point doing this task if we use bad English to do it.*
TEACHER: *I couldn't disagree more. If you were stuck in a strange English town and you needed to find a hotel for the night would it be more important to you to speak perfect English but not communicate or to communicate successfully but in English that had a few mistakes? Achieving success in a task using your English is a huge achievement. Speaking 'perfect' English is something else – something to work on, but not essential. It's much more important to work first on getting your message across.*

To summarize the teacher's arguments:

- There are times in class when a focus on accuracy (and therefore a greater use of instant correction) is appropriate.
- There are other times when the focus is on fluency. At these times instant correction is less appropriate and could interfere with the aims of the activity.
- The teacher needs to be clear about whether her main aim is accuracy or fluency, and adapt her role in class appropriately. ■

Task 2

What is the teacher's role likely to be in an activity mainly geared towards encouraging fluency? Imagine yourself in the classroom while the students are doing the activity. Where are you? What are you doing? How 'involved' are you?

Commentary ■ ■ ■

If the main aim is to get the *students* to speak, then one way to help that would be for teachers to reduce their own contributions. Probably the less they speak, the more space it will allow the students. It could be useful to aim to say nothing while the activity is underway, and save any contributions for before and after.

Similarly, getting out of the way might be a help. If I stay at the front of the class, visible and clearly keeping an eye over everything, that might put students off talking. I might do well to slink away into a quiet back corner of the room and watch with interest, but unobtrusively.

≪ The experiential learning cycle p 3

The more 'present' I allow myself to be, the more likely I am to feel that I need to intervene or the more likely students will be to ask me for help. And the more I help, the more I make the task less challenging for the students, the more they will lean on me. The more involved I get, the more I end up doing the communication rather than them. Active 'not helping' may sound rather cruel, but I think there are times when the teacher can be most helpful by forcing students to face problems themselves.

Thus, a basic procedure for a communicative activity might be:

1 Teacher introduces and sets up activity (teacher centre-stage).
2 Students do activity (teacher out of sight, uninvolved).
3 Teacher gets feedback, does follow-on work, etc (teacher centre-stage again).

A useful thing for the teacher to do during stage 2 above is to take notes (unobtrusively) of interesting student utterances (correct and incorrect) for possible use later on (at the end of the activity, the next day, next week, etc).

Some ideas for correction work after a fluency activity:

- The teacher writes up a number of sentences used during the activity and discusses them with the students.
- The teacher writes a number of sentences on the board. She gives the pens/chalks to the students and encourages them to make corrections.
- The teacher invents and writes out a story that includes a number of errors she overheard during the activity. She hands out the story the next day and the students, in pairs or as a whole group, attempt to find the errors and correct them.
- The teacher writes out two lists headed 'A' and 'B'. On each list she writes the same ten sentences from the activity. On one list she writes the sentence with an error; on the other she writes the corrected version. Thus the correct version of sentence 3 might be on either list 'A' or list 'B' and the other list has an error.

The teacher divides the students into two groups, 'A' and 'B', and hands out the appropriate list to each group. The groups discuss their own list (without sight of the other list) and try to decide if their version of each sentence is correct or not. If it is wrong they correct it. When they have discussed all the sentences, the groups can then compare the two sheets (and perhaps come to some new conclusions). ■

>> Errors and correction p 109

4   Drama and roleplay

Drama is an excellent way to get students using the language. It essentially involves using the imagination to make oneself into another character, or the classroom into a different place. It can be a starting point for exciting listening and speaking work and it can be utilized as a tool to provide practice in specific grammatical, lexical, functional or phonological areas.

By bringing the outside world into the classroom in this way we can provide a lot of useful practice (in cafes, shops, banks, businesses, streets, parties, etc) that would otherwise be impossible. There can also be a freeing from the constraints of culture and expected behaviour; this can be personally and linguistically very liberating. Curiously, it is sometimes the shyest students who are most able to seize the potential.

Success or failure of drama activities depends crucially on the perceived attitude of the teacher and of the other students; without a certain degree of trust, acceptance and respect the chances for useful work are greatly diminished.

Six types of drama activity are commonly found in English language teaching classrooms:

- **Roleplay.** Students act out small scenes using their own ideas or from ideas and information on role-cards.
- **Simulation.** This is really a large-scale roleplay. Role-cards are normally used and there is often other background information as well. The intention is to create a much more complete, complex 'world', say of a business company, television studio, government body, etc.
- **Drama games.** Short games that usually involve movement and imagination.
- **Guided improvisation.** A scene is improvised. One by one the students join in in character, until the whole scene and possibly story take on a life of their own.
- **Acting play scripts.** Short written sketches or scenes are acted by the students.
- **Prepared improvised drama.** Students in small groups invent and rehearse a short scene or story that they then perform for the others.

The following pages look at roleplay, drama games and guided improvisation.

Task 1

Here are three role-cards. A fourth card is missing. Write it.

> You are a store detective. You can see a suspicious-looking person at a clothes rail who appears to be putting something into her bag. Go over and firmly but politely ask her to come to the office.

> You bought a sweater from this shop yesterday but you have brought it back, because it is too small. You want to go to the assistant to return it and get your money back, but before you do, you start looking at the other sweaters on the rail and comparing them with the one you got yesterday, which is in your bag.

> You are a shop assistant. You have just noticed a customer coming in who was very rude to you yesterday. She wanted to buy a sweater, which you told her was the wrong size, but she insisted was right. Finally she stormed out without buying it. You hope she isn't going to cause more trouble.

Commentary ■ ■ ■

Possibly:

> You are the manager of a large department store. The police have just phoned you to warn that a number of shop-lifters are operating in this street. You decide to have a walk around your store and warn the assistants and the store detective to keep their eyes open.

This roleplay provides the possibility of practising 'shop' vocabulary in a useful and interesting way. There is also a lot of scope for use of functional language – apologizing, refusing, disagreeing, denying, etc. The potential for dramatic conflict is built into the cards, though the participants could, if they wished, avoid this completely.

Running a roleplay: some guidelines

- Make sure the students understand the idea of 'roleplay'. Do they know what's going to happen? Do they know what is required of them? Are they comfortable to do that or not?
- Make sure the context or situation is clear.
- Do they understand the information on their own card? Allow reading time, dictionary time, thinking time (during which you can go round and help if necessary).
- Give them time to prepare their ideas before the speaking starts; maybe encourage note-making.
- ... but when the activity starts, encourage them to improvise rather than rely on prepared speeches and notes. The preparation work they have done will inform their roleplay, but could simply get in the way if they over-rely on it. (It may help to *take away* the cards when the roleplay starts.)

Drama games

Here are four short examples:

Walking

A good way to 'become' another character is to try to walk in the way they would. This also makes an interesting short drama game in its own right. The students stand up and walk around the room, as a character of their choice. After a while, various people can meet each other and have short conversations (eg Marilyn Monroe meeting Shakespeare). Variation 1: the teacher calls out names of characters from a story, or the news or history, etc and the students all try to act in character. Variation 2: the students must walk in the manner of the word: for example, *happy, young, tired, cold, tense*.

Making a picture

The teacher calls out a subject; the students must all together quickly form a frozen 'tableau' of that scene. For example: the teacher calls out *airport*; the students take different positions. Some are check-in clerks, some become desks, some become planes taking off, some become tourists, until the whole room 'becomes' an airport. An amusing variation is to divide the class in two. One half has two minutes to make their scene, while the other waits outside the room or in another room. When they return to view the tableau they must guess what the scene is. They are only allowed to ask questions that would have yes/no answers (eg *Are you a table? No. Are you holding something? Yes.*).

Puppets and dubbing

Puppets: Two people (A and B) sit. Two other people (C and D) sit directly behind them. A and B now hide their arms behind their backs while C and D put their arms out in front, so that they look as if they are A and B's real arms. A and B attempt to carry on a conversation while C and D move their arms and hands appropriately. Can be hilarious!

Dubbing: This time C and D sit slightly to one side of A and B. They provide the words that A and B speak by whispering into their ears. A and B are not allowed to say anything except what they are told to say.

Interesting situations

Students call out any interesting or 'difficult' situation involving two people and two other students act it out. For example, a well-meaning hostess serving meat to a polite vegetarian. This technique could, in appropriate circumstances, be used to 'real-play' (ie act out and explore some of the students' own real-life problem situations).

Guided improvisation

The teacher selects a scene – say, a frozen winter landscape with a frozen lake. The idea is to turn the classroom into the scene, and to then let the story unfold in any way it can, by the group improvising together.

The teacher might start by describing the scene and getting students to become people in the landscape, slowly building up a living, moving scene, or he might jump in the deep end by adopting a character himself and encouraging others to join him in the improvisation as and when they are ready.

The skill of running this kind of complex improvisation is to find a balance between allowing a free-flowing, growing, alive improvisation and the necessity of keeping some control over it to ensure that it keeps momentum and avoids silliness or trite solutions. Most of the teacher's interventions to achieve this can be done subtly by saying something, in character, to some of the participants, rather than by stepping in and making grand announcements to everyone.

Some ideas for guided improvisations:

- the perfect school
- a museum (or waxworks) at night
- the beach
- inside a plane
- kitchen implements come alive
- an amazing party
- the secret life of the characters in your coursebook

Task 2

Devise either role-cards or a basic scenario for a guided improvisation to enable students to practise the language of asking for and giving instructions (eg finding out how to use a new machine, play a new game, etc).

Answer to *splurg* puzzle (p 66)
Splurgs are vacuum cleaners or 'Hoovers'.
The last five sentences are untrue.
The spy novel referred to is *Our Man in Havana* by Graham Greene.

Acknowledgement
The inspiration for this activity came from 'Plogs' in *Keep Talking* by F. Klippel (CUP 1984).

---

c Give clear acknowledgement or feedback to each student utterance. You could use simple gestures or facial expressions or short comments such as *thank you, good, yes,* etc.

d If someone gives an incorrect answer get them to repeat it two or three times and then say the correct answer yourself.

e If they can't provide an answer don't stretch the eliciting out too long. Silence or wrong answers are evidence that they *need* your input.

f When you have an appropriate answer, make sure it is clearly established as a good answer, perhaps by getting it repeated by a variety of individuals.

g Don't use elicitation with monolingual classes.

h Use elicitation regularly as a basic technique in most lessons for keeping your class active and involved.

Answers

d and **g** are the foxes in the henhouse!

Task 2

Today's lesson will work on language used when meeting people at parties. What questions could you ask at the start of your lesson in order to interest the learners and to elicit some of their personal feelings and reactions?

Task 3

Consider the next lesson you need to teach. Write down one specific item of factual information that the students will need to know – maybe a grammar rule, a fact about the topic, what a picture on the board represents, etc. Write a *sequence* of questions that you could use to lead the students step by step towards finding out that same information for themselves.

If possible, work with someone else to try out your sequence of questions. Practise drawing out the information rather than explaining yourself.

6   Fingers

Carry them around with you at all times! Put a few in your pocket for emergencies!

This section introduces a simple but effective basic technique for clarifying the structure of sentences and for instant error correction – especially useful when you are working mainly on spoken English without immediate use of written models. For example, you're teaching *He went to Milan yesterday,* and one of your learners is confused about the word order.

Basic technique

- Put down any pens, paper, etc you have and hold up one hand in front of you.
- Each finger represents one word. Use your other hand to point to (or indicate) each word/finger in turn as you say the sentence (or you elicit the sentence from the students) – see Fig. 8.4 on p 102.
- The learner gets a clear visual indication of the shape of the sentence.

Fig. 8.4

(nb the word order for your students must read left to right – so from your position behind the fingers, the sentence will appear to be right to left.)

Students may need a little 'training' before this technique shows its real simplicity and power. The first time you use 'finger sentences' make sure your learners are clear that fingers represent words. Don't let them rush you; allow time to focus clearly on the individual words/fingers and clarify the problem they have. Once learners have seen the technique used three or four times, it soon becomes a valuable classroom tool.

Variations and ideas

A learner says a sentence wrongly. The teacher gets her to repeat the sentence while he indicates with his fingers each word as it is said. When the error is reached the teacher indicates that this word is the problem by facial expression or a gesture. The teacher can then clarify the error by means of more specific signs:

a These two words are in the wrong order.
See Fig. 8.5.

b You don't need this word.
Fold down the finger corresponding to the extra word.

c There should be an extra word here.
Point to the gap between the appropriate fingers.

d Say it quickly.
Hold out spread fingers, and with the other hand close them together.

e Third syllable is wrong.
Use the joints of your finger to represent the syllables.

f Contraction (eg *I am > I'm*).
Hold the appropriate fingers apart and then move them together.

Fig. 8.5: Pinpointing the error: these two words are in the wrong order

Task 1

Practise this with a colleague facing you (or a mirror if there are no volunteers around). Take a sentence in a foreign language or a nonsense sentence (eg *pop tee tipple on ug*). Say the sentence quickly – get your colleague to repeat it. Then use the techniques above to get them (a) to improve their pronunciation of individual words and the whole sentence, and then (b) to learn a question form.

7　Time lines

These are a tool for clarifying the 'time' of various verb tenses. A time line attempts to make the flow of time visible, and thus enable learners to see more clearly exactly how one tense differs from another, or how a single tense can refer to different 'times'.

The starting point is a line representing time. On this line we need to mark *now* – the precise present moment. From the left, time flows from the past towards *now*. To the right of this, time flows into the future.

Past　　　　　　　　　　　Now　　　　　　Future

So, for example, *I'm drinking a glass of lemonade* refers to something happening *now*, that started just before now, and finishes just after now.

We can mark it:

In contrast, *I drank a glass of lemonade last night* might be shown:

And, *I'm going to drink a glass of lemonade:*

Unfortunately, the appealing clarity of a diagram like these may be an over-simplification. English verb forms tell us about more than just the time something happened. *I'm going to drink a glass of lemonade*, for example, suggests a decision to drink made *before now*, which we can show as:

It also includes a sense of the speaker speaking now and looking forward to the future:

Which time line is the most truthful? Which most helpful to learners? You'll have to decide for yourself.

Some tenses are quite difficult to diagrammatize – the present perfect progressive, for example:

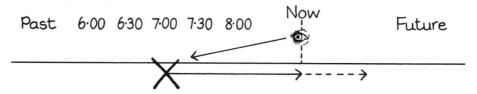

I've been waiting since 7.00. The diagram shows that we are looking back into the past to the time the waiting started. It shows us that the waiting has continued up to 'now'. It also shows that there is a possibility it could continue into the future.

We can also show the relationship between two or more different tenses:

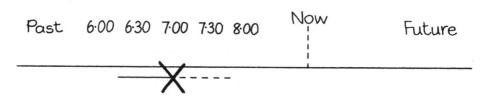

I was cooking supper when the cooker exploded. One action (that might have continued) has been interrupted by another (past continuous interrupted by simple past).

Time lines are one way of making English grammar more accessible. But do remember that their meaning and use may not be transparently clear to everyone. Some learners may be as much confused or puzzled by them as enlightened. Use them to help yourself clarify the meaning of tenses and then to help your learners. When you are asked for an explanation of the meaning of a verb tense, try putting a time line on the board as a visual aid. Ask questions; invite ideas. Use time lines as a cue for elicitation. Get students to draw time lines for themselves to help check understanding. Invite students to the board to work out time lines together. Adapt time lines and personalize them to suit your own approach (some people use colours; some draw little people all over them; etc). As we have seen, there is not necessarily one right answer.

« Eliciting p 99

« Meaning p 75

» Concept questions p 126

Time lines are one way of becoming clearer about meaning. For another useful idea see the sections on concept and concept questions.

Task 1

Using a grammar book to help you if you want, (1) name the tenses and (2) make time lines for:

a I used to live in Nairobi.
b I live in Nairobi.
c I'm living in Nairobi.
d I was walking past the station.
e I heard the explosion.
f I was walking past the station when I heard the explosion.
g Bob cooked lunch while they were sleeping.
h While they were sleeping, Bob was cooking the lunch.
i Have you been to Thailand?
j He's just walked in the door.
k I'd hidden the money before she came in.

See p 113 for sketches of answers.

8 Fillers

Most teachers find they need a small collection of 'fillers' – things to do when they've run out of other things to do, perhaps because the main activity went much faster than expected and (even having stretched it) there is still a seven-minute gap at the end of the lesson before the bell rings. Fillers are also useful at the start of a lesson as a warmer (particularly when you are waiting for some latecomers) or mid-lesson as a way of changing the pace, or of breaking up similar activities. Fillers may be quite separate from the surrounding lesson or they might connect in some way. They are often useful as a chance to recycle vocabulary from earlier lessons. They are often an opportunity to work on activities that have a 'group-building' aim rather than a purely language aim.

» Word games p 107

Fillers might be: word games, other games (especially team games), stories, puzzles, physical games and exercises, music or songs.

» Storytelling p 173

» Songs and music p 176

I suggest you aim to get together a list of your own favourite fillers (and prepare any necessary material); file these in a handy place, at the front of a course file for example, so that in an emergency you can quickly look at the list and be reminded of the likely choices.

Here are a few much-used fillers:

Revision dictation

Divide the class into teams. Choose between five and fifteen sentences (or words) from the lesson. Dictate these, challenging the teams to write down the sentences/words with correct spelling. Allow them time for arguing and agreeing. At the end, go through the whole list. Give points for completely correct answers.

Yes and *no* questions

Quick story puzzles often go down well. Describe a slightly cryptic basic situation or problem (perhaps an incident from your own life); the learners have to question you further, discuss and find a solution that explains the story. You can only answer *yes* or *no* to any questions asked. Example: *A stranger crawled all over my sitting room today.* (Answer: I'd dropped a contact lens; the TV repair man helped me find it.) There are some famous examples. This seems to be the favourite: *Feargal McDonald lived on the twentieth floor of a block of flats and every morning took the lift down to the ground floor and caught the bus into town. When he came home he took the lift to the seventh floor and then climbed the stairs all the way to the twentieth floor. Why?* (Answer: he was a schoolboy and couldn't reach the lift control buttons higher than floor seven.) And I like this one: *A man is pushing a car on a road. When he gets to the hotel he will lose all his money. What's happening?* (Answer: it's a game of Monopoly.)

The hotel receptionist game

Prepare a list of likely (and unlikely) sentences that a guest would say to a hotel receptionist (eg *What time is breakfast? Where's the restaurant? My TV has exploded, I've lost my wallet.*) Hand one of these sentences to a student who must mime it well enough for the class to guess the original sentence. Could be a team game with points. Could use other situations such as *airport, theatre, family at dinner*, etc.

Kim's game

Prepare a tray with about twenty to thirty small objects on it (eg pencil, cassette, paperback, comb, etc). Show it to the students for two minutes, then cover it (or remove the tray from sight). The students must make a list (as individuals or in teams) of all the objects they can remember. The winner is the one who gets most. (Could be done with a list of words on the board, or with flashcards if you can't get enough objects.)

Ordering

Instruct students to stand in line according to their birth month and date (ie Jan 1 stands far left, Dec 31 on right). They will need to discuss and rearrange themselves a little. Once they have got the idea of organizing themselves in this way you can try some other instructions: for example, by alphabetical order of first name; by first letter of your favourite hobby; by distance lived from school (furthest to closest); by how much you like sport (most to least), etc.

Change of mood

Put on some likely music. Lead (or get a student to volunteer to lead) a four-minute relaxation/aerobic/exercise session. (Be sure that you know your class and their likely reaction before you try out something like this. In any case it's probably better to 'invite' participation rather than to 'demand' it.)

Paintbox

Assign one of three or four colours to each student in the class – eg green, red, blue, orange. Arrange the seating in a circle so that there is *one less* seat than the people present. The leftover person stands in the middle. He must call out a colour – eg *Green*. At this all *green* students must stand up and find another seat for themselves. They cannot sit down in the same seat that they have just left. The person in the middle is also using this opportunity to find a vacant seat for himself. Whoever is left seatless at the end continues the game by calling out a new colour. She also has the option of calling 'Paintbox,' in which case *everyone* must move and find a new seat! Lots of movement and happy chaos. Watch out that it doesn't get too rough; the game should be played with 'cat-like' stealth rather than rugby tackles.

This popular movement game has many names and variations – I've heard it called 'Fruit salad' and 'The wind blows'. It's easy to see how it can be adapted. The vocabulary area could be changed to offer practice in many different areas, eg fruit, grammatical terms, clothes, etc. We could also personalize it: *All people wearing white socks change places, All people who arrived late to this lesson change places,* etc.

A song

>> Songs and music p 176   Choose a song and make a copy of the text with a number of missing words. In class, the students listen to the song and attempt to fill in the missing words.

Task 1

Recall a game you have played outside the classroom. What adaptations or variations would you need in order to make it into a classroom activity?

9   Word games

Many well-known word games can be used in the classroom as fillers or as integrated practice activities. Perhaps the most popular one is Hangman (I prefer variations where something a little less gruesome happens) but many other word games are possible. Here are five I have found useful:

Word jumbles (or Word clouds or Word pools)

Take a number of words that the class has met over the previous lesson or two and write them up on the board with their letters mixed up. The learners try to decipher them. (Possibly the words when rearranged could then be formed into a sentence?)

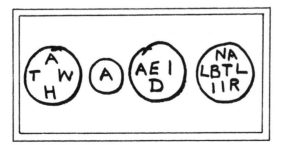

I went into town

This is a useful game for revising vocabulary and is especially good for work on countable and uncountable nouns. In this example the teacher has specified 'food' as the vocabulary area. The first learner says *I went into town and I bought an apple.* The next learner must repeat the sentence and add a second item beginning with the next letter of the alphabet, eg *I went into town and I bought an apple and a banana.* The third then says *I went into town and I bought an apple, a banana and some carrots,* etc. Make the rest of the rules up yourself!

Instant crossword

Ask the class to look back over words that they have studied in the last two or three days. Get them to shout out two to you and write them clearly on the board, interlocking, as in a crossword puzzle.

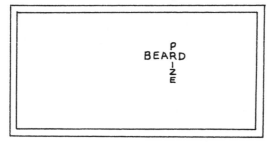

This could now continue as a competitive team game (teams take it in turns to add a new word to the grid) or as a class effort, trying to make the grid as big as possible. The students could take over the writing once the rules have been established.

It might help to divide the board up into squares beforehand, though the game works well enough without, so long as the writing is clear.

Don't finish a word

The class is divided into two teams. Each team takes it in turns to call out a letter, which is written on the board. They also say whether their letter goes *in front of* or *behind* the letters already on the board. Thus the chain of letters on the board grows longer turn by turn. If (a) a team thinks the previous team has finished a complete word or (b) a team thinks the previous team could not possibly make a word from the letters now on the board, then they 'challenge' (ie you must always have a word in mind when you place a new letter). A correct challenge wins the round.

Example 1

Team 1:	*B*	
Team 2:	*BA*	
Team 1:	*BAC*	(Thinking of *back*)
Team 2:	*OBAC*	
Team 1:	*Challenge*	(They think team 2 is bluffing and cannot possibly make a word from these letters.)
Team 2:	*TOBACCO*	(And wins the round.)

Example 2

Team 2:	*N*	
Team 1:	*AN*	
Team 2:	*Challenge*	(They win - it's a complete word.)

Making use of ARC as a descriptive tool

The three **ARC** components can be used to describe many different kinds of lessons, both successful and problematic. Even though we have so far looked at only four basic lesson types, it is clearly already possible to devise variations on and additions to these types, for example turning **CRRA** into **CRRRRAA** or **CA**. **ARC** is a simple descriptive tool for preparing lessons, and a useful objective instrument for describing what actually happens in the classroom.

By placing the three **ARC** components in order we can give a simple description of a lesson. A more complete description of a lesson is possible if we include details of which skill areas are involved in the **A** and **R** categories, and information about how **C** (the clarification and focus) was done. This information could be noted when writing down the **ARC** sequence. For example:

R (writing); **C** (students read coursebook); **R** (writing).

Alternatively, a form such as the one below could be used.

ARC	Skill area/further details	Time
A	Introduction/scene setting	2 mins
R	Written exercise	12 mins
C	Students read coursebook explanation	5 mins
R	Written exercise	11 mins

Fig. 9.4: ARC form

A descriptive analysis such as this allows us to consider the overall shape of a lesson and the balance of activities within it. In the example in Fig. 9.4, the analysis is similar to the type 4 lesson above, but here the emphasis is clearly on written practice, rather than reading or speaking. The limited **A** (Authentic use) is also apparent. A lesson such as this may be useful and appropriate for certain classes on certain occasions. However, an analysis over a series of lessons that produced similar descriptions would show up a noticeable deficiency in the work being done.

Task 3

Here are three further examples of problematic lessons. Match the **ARC** sequence to the lesson descriptions.

> **AAAAA**
> **RRRRRRR**
> **CCCC**

1 The teacher explained at length, and at random, a number of different grammar points until the bell rang.
2 A teacher on a lazy day didn't know what he was doing until he came into the room, opened the grammar workbook and said *Do exercise 1, 2, 3 etc.*
3 An untrained teacher thought he was being lively and modern by doing a whole series of communicative activities one after the other and then setting an essay.

Answers
1C 2R 3A

Commentary ■ ■ ■

By clearly describing lessons in this manner, noting the **ARC** sequence and the skills areas, omissions and sequencing problems can become much clearer. Lesson 3, for example, may have been useful, but the lack of **C** (Clarification and focus) or **R** (Restricted use activities) is apparent, and if the teacher used this type of sequence regularly, then the students would certainly be missing out on some important things. ■

Although we have so far only considered a few lessons, note that the order of the three components is quite different in each. There are certainly many other possible orders as well.

7   Analyzing language: communicative function

It is possible to speak English that is grammatically correct, yet is still wrong.

Task 1

What is the problem in these situations?

a A foreign student staying as a guest with an English family says *I want breakfast at seven o'clock. I want two sandwiches and a cup of chocolate.*

b Student 2 stops someone in the street and asks *What have you got on your watch?*·

Commentary ■ ■ ■

Although each sentence is grammatically correct, each seems wrong in a different way. We use language to express meanings, and the language we use is different in different situations and with different people. What is correct and suitable in one set of circumstances is partially or completely inappropriate in another. Example **a** might just be acceptable in a hotel, but as a guest in a family it is plain rude.

We might ask a friend to *Pass us that newspaper, will you?* but to a stranger in the dentist's waiting room we are more likely to say, *Excuse me. Could you pass me that copy of* The Times? Knowing the grammar of the language backwards is often little help in forming expressions such as these; students need to discover what is appropriate in a particular situation. They also need to learn some complete fixed expressions. Thus, for example, in **b** *Have you got the time on you?* or *Can you tell me the time?* would be correct. ■

A grammatical analysis of English divides the language up into separate grammatical items. Alternatively, we can divide the language up in a completely different way – in terms of 'communicative function' – the language we use to express particular ideas or to achieve particular results in particular situations. We are looking at the *purpose* of an utterance rather than analyzing its component pieces. The sentences or examples of language used are known as 'exponents' of a function. Thus *Have you got the time on you?* is an exponent of the function of 'asking for information'. Some exponents are fixed formulae that allow for little or no alteration: you cannot change any word in *Have you got the time on you?* without losing the meaning. Other exponents have more generative possibilities: *Could you tell me the way to the station?* is usable in a variety of situations by substituting different vocabulary for *station*.

Task 2

Match the functions below with the exponents on the right. There may be none, one, or more than one exponent under each heading.

Giving instructions

Refusing

Apologizing

Disagreeing

Put it in the bag.
Thanks, but I can't.
I don't think you're right.
Surely not!
Well, to my mind, the UN has the best chance.
I'm awfully sorry.
We regret any inconvenience caused.
I do apologize.
No. I won't.
Write the answer in your book.

Task 3

Here are some exponents. Name the function.

I wish I'd done it; If only I hadn't gone there; Why didn't I buy it when I had the chance?

Answer
The function is 'expressing regret'.

Task 4

How important are stress and intonation to the correct use of the exponents in Tasks 2 and 3?

Commentary ■ ■ ■

Stress and intonation are very important. A change of stress and intonation can make an exponent change its function. For example, *I'm awfully sorry* could be a genuine apology or a sarcastic expression of anger.

A lot of work in the area of function is to do with common sense and common politeness – and most of all to do with an awareness of audience. This, of course, is partly cultural. We can help students become more aware of appropriacy by getting them to consider:

- Who are you talking/writing to? How well do you know them?
- How formal/informal is the relationship?
- Where are you? What unwritten rules or codes of conduct apply?

Some ideas for integrating functional work into a course:

- focusing on a functional area and studying a number of exponents;
- roleplays – considering what to say in particular relationships;
- listening – working out relationships between speakers;
- deciding how different situations make one sentence mean different things;
- building dialogues and picture story conversations;
- acting out play scripts;
- writing letters to different people;
- altering written conversations to change the relationship. ■

《 Drama and roleplay p 69

《 Drama and roleplay p 69
》 Ideas for writing tasks p 162

Task 5

What is the relationship of the speakers in the following conversation? Keeping as much of the original meaning as possible, change the dialogue to make it sound like a natural exchange between (a) two close friends; (b) parent and young child.

A: I'm sorry to interrupt, but I was wondering whether you wanted to break for lunch yet?

B: I'm afraid I'm still rather busy. But thank you very much for asking.

A: Perhaps I'll see you in the restaurant later.

B: Yes. That would be nice.

8   Phonology: the sounds of English

The phonological system of English can be divided into five main areas: the individual sounds; word stress; sentence stress; intonation; and features of fluent connected speech. This section is an introduction to sounds, stress and intonation.

Sounds

Task 1

The phonemic chart in Fig. 9.5 shows the individual sounds ('phonemes') of the English language. Referring to a dictionary that uses the IPA (international phonetic alphabet), find out which phoneme is represented by the letters underlined in the following words.

Vowels
sch<u>oo</u>ls <u>au</u>tonomy p<u>a</u>rticipation co-<u>o</u>peration v<u>a</u>luing tr<u>u</u>st <u>i</u>n l<u>ear</u>ners' resp<u>e</u>ct th<u>e</u>* g<u>oo</u>d t<u>ea</u>chers

*be careful: how does this sound in a normally spoken sentence?

Diphthongs
<u>air</u> j<u>oy</u> h<u>o</u>peful gr<u>ea</u>t br<u>igh</u>t p<u>ure</u> cl<u>ear</u> s<u>ou</u>nds

Consonants
<u>w</u>ashing machine <u>y</u>east <u>p</u>otatoes <u>b</u>eans <u>kn</u>ives si<u>n</u>k <u>h</u>erbs* tomatoes bro<u>th</u>erliness fore<u>s</u>ight vi<u>s</u>ion brea<u>d</u> <u>ch</u>eese <u>fr</u>iendliness sensiti<u>v</u>ity <u>j</u>am <u>c</u>ake e<u>gg</u>s empa<u>thy</u> <u>fr</u>idge food mi<u>x</u>er kett<u>le</u> wi<u>s</u>dom compa<u>ss</u>ion

*UK pronunciation

For commentary on this task see p 144.

Students of most other foreign languages will find that, while a number of English phonemes are familiar, some will be distinctly different from ones they use. Particular problems arise when:

- English has two phonemes for a sound that seems to an untrained ear to be a single sound. A common example of this is the distinction between /ɪ/ and /iː/ (as in *hip* vs *heap*), which to some students sound the same;
- English has a phoneme that does not exist in the student's own language.

In both cases, getting students to produce the sounds themselves can be difficult; it is necessary to raise their awareness of the fact that there is something to work on, and the first step is to get them to *hear* the difference. Receptive awareness comes before productive competence.

iː	ɪ	ʊ	uː	ɪə	eɪ	✗
e	ə	ɜː	ɔː	ʊə	ɔɪ	əʊ
æ	ʌ	ɑː	ɒ	eə	aɪ	aʊ
p	b	t	d	tʃ	dʒ	k	g
f	v	θ	ð	s	z	ʃ	ʒ
m	n	ŋ	h	l	r	w	j

Fig. 9.5: Phonemic chart

Some ideas for working with phonemes:

- Integrate phonemic work into your teaching of grammar and vocabulary. Always work on helping the students to achieve good pronunciation and encourage them to make a record of the phonemic transcription as well as the spelling of new items.
- Observation of mechanics. Let students watch how you and they make particular sounds.
- Ear-training. Get students to listen to and distinguish words which have sounds that seem to them very similar (eg hat vs hut; thin vs tin. Examples of this kind are known as *minimal pairs*).
- Tongue twisters – to work on particular sounds, or to contrast sounds (eg three thin trees and three tall trees).
- Transliteration. Get students to write out a word or sentence in phonemic script. Jokes seem to work well.
- Using a dictionary to find pronunciation.
- Phoneme bingo. Hand out bingo cards with phonemes instead of numbers; call out sounds rather than numbers.
- Tap out words on a phonemic chart or using phonemes written on the board – students say the words.
- Try a phonemic crossword like the one below.

Task 2

1		2	▓	3		4
	▓	5			▓	
6			▓	7		

Across

1 past of 1 down
3 some teachers do this too much!
5 soldiers work for this organization
6 past of 7 across
7 '_____ here!'

Down

1 '_____ your time!'
2 no movement; still
3 a clock makes this noise
4 you use this to make your hair tidy

For the answers, see p 145.

Word stress

A stressed syllable in a word is usually noticeable by being slightly louder, slightly longer and slightly higher in pitch than the syllables next to it.

Task 3

There are a variety of ways of marking stress in a written text. Which of the following do you personally find clearest?

formation;   'window   unhȧppy   **wat**erfall

ca|ssette| impostor   de^light~ful~   magaZINE

Task 4

Mark the stressed syllable in the following words using the method you chose in Task 3.

photograph   photographer   telescope   telescopic

underwater   chemical   computer   forest

dictionary   comfortable   reception

For the answers, see p 145.

Word stress is important because when it is wrong, words sound very strange or even incomprehensible. Would anyone understand you saying: sec**ret**ary?

Sometimes wrong stress changes one word into another: **de**sert   de**sert**

Task 5

Put the words into the correct columns.

interview   computer

revision   dictionary

underground   innocent

completely   important

suitable   example

recorder   universe

opposite

For the answers, see p 145.

The kinds of tasks given so far in this section are also very useful for your students to work with. As with work on the sounds of English, awareness itself is an essential starting point and it is worth devising tasks and activities that assist this.

Sentence stress

Although individual words have their own stress, stress is also an important feature of sentences. Sentences usually have at least one main stress, and probably a number of secondary ones. Changes in sentence stress make substantial differences to meaning.

Task 6

In the following sentence underline any syllables that could be stressed.

Caroline's going to fly to Africa on Tuesday.

For an answer, see p 145.

Stress typically marks out the content-carrying words in the sentence – thus it mostly affects nouns, verbs and adjectives. One important effect of sentence stress is to mark out a rhythm. There is also a dramatic effect on unstressed words in a sentence. Note, for example, the difference between the pronunciation of *to* when said on its own compared with how it appears in the example sentence above (/tuː/ vs /tə/).

Unstressed words tend to be pronounced quite fast, almost as if trying to cram themselves into the spaces between the beats of the rhythm (a common feature of student English is a failure to do this – giving each word in the sentence equal time in the rhythm). They also tend to be pronounced in a 'weak' manner; they typically use shorter vowel sounds: /ə/ rather than /uː/; /ɪ/ rather than /iː/, etc). This use of weak forms is one of the features of connected speech that makes comprehension more difficult for students. If you are expecting to hear *to* pronounced as /tuː/ or *was* pronounced as /wɒz/, then you are less likely to recognize the words when you hear /tə/ or /wəz/. The most common weak form vowel sound (and thus the most common sound in the English language) is /ə/ – the *schwa*.

Task 7

At random, choose a sentence from anywhere in this book. Mark every schwa in it.

Task 8

Consider the effect that changing stress has on the meaning of a single sentence. Finish the explanatory notes in the same way as the first example.

a Michael wanted to buy the red **shirt**.   (not the red jumper)

b Michael wanted to **buy** the red shirt.   (not …

c **Michael** wanted to buy the red shirt.   (not …

d Michael wanted to buy the **red** shirt.   (not …

e Michael **wanted** to buy the red shirt.   (but …

For the answers, see p 145.

We can demonstrate the patterns of sentence stress on the board, or by using Cuisenaire rods, or by tapping, clapping, humming the rhythm, etc. By getting the students to work out the patterns themselves we can help to make them more aware of the importance of stress. Poetry and songs are good for focusing on stress. Shadow reading (reading simultaneously with a tape, trying to keep up with the speed and follow the rhythm) is a useful language laboratory or classroom activity.

Intonation

Intonation is sometimes referred to as the 'music' of the language, and we use it as a kind of oral equivalent of written punctuation. It is closely connected to sentence stress, for the main movement of intonation begins at a stress. This movement is either upwards (a *rise*), or downwards (a *fall*), or flat. Intonation has a definite effect on meaning and also gives us information about the speaker's attitude.

It is hard to teach intonation systematically because, although there are some common patterns, there are few clear rules, and many people with an 'unmusical' ear find it very hard to recognize or categorize intonation patterns. It is, however, so important that it is essential to include work on intonation in most courses. Many learners speak English with a *flat* intonation, which can sound boring, bored or uninterested. Using wrong intonation can also give offence.

Some ideas for working on intonation:

- Get students to mark intonation patterns on dialogues. (How can you mark it? Arrows? Lines? Music? Write the words in a wiggly way to reflect the movement?)
- Get students to say the same single word (eg hello) with different intonation to convey completely different meanings.
- Hum/whistle/sing the sentence without words before you say it.
- Indicate intonation with hand gestures, waves, etc.
- Exaggerate intonation (this can be very funny).
- Exaggerate lack of intonation.
- Encourage students to 'feel' the emotion as they speak. Emotions of anger, interest, surprise, boredom, etc can naturally power the intonation.

Task 9

Add the words *fall* or *rise* to the following guidelines:

a *Wh-* questions (ie *Where ... Who ... What ...*, etc) usually ...
b Questions that are answered *yes/no* usually ...
c Orders usually ...

For the answers, see p 145.

Answers to tasks

Task 1, p 140

You'll have noticed that the words come together to make complete sentences or lexical sets. You may find a mnemonic of some kind helpful while you are learning the phonemes. Your students might also like this idea: you could write a simple story for them (eg 'Eat this good food,' said the girl ...) or, better still, get them to devise their own sentences. You could also attempt more 'poetic' versions.

Vowels

Teachers in good schools respect the learners' autonomy, valuing trust, participation, co-operation.

Diphthongs

clear pure air; great joy; bright hopeful sounds

Consonants

First row: food

potatoes; beans; tomatoes; bread; cheese; jam; cake; eggs

Second row: positive human characteristics

friendliness; sensitivity; empathy; brotherliness; foresight; wisdom; compassion; vision

Third row: words associated with kitchens

food mixer; knives; sink; herbs; kettle; fridge; washing machine; yeast

Task 2, p 141

¹ t ʊ k	² k		³ t ɔː	⁴ k	
eɪ		⁵ ɑː m	ɪ		əʊ
⁶ k eɪ m			⁷ k ʌ m		

Task 4, p 142

PHOtograph   phoTOgrapher   TELescope   teleSCOpic

underWAter   CHEmical   comPUter   FOrest

DICtionary   COMfortable   reCEPtion

Task 5, p 142

■ ▪ ▪	▪ ■ ▪
interview	revision
underground	completely
suitable	recorder
opposite	computer
dictionary	important
innocent	example
universe	

Task 6, p 143

Any of the underlined syllables might be stressed:

Caroline's going to fly to Africa on Tuesday.

The speaker's choice as to her intended meaning will determine which syllable carries the most stress. (See Task 8 below.)

Task 8, p 143

b not steal/borrow, etc.
c not Fred/Jane/Susan, etc.

d not the green/blue one, etc.
e but he didn't.

Task 9, p 144

a fall   **b** rise   **c** fall

Chapter 10   # Language skills

Introduction

We have already looked at the skill of speaking in Chapter 6. In this chapter we
consider the other three language skills: listening, reading and writing.

1   Task-based listening: an introduction

We can use listening work in the classroom as one way to help focus on language
systems (eg grammar or vocabulary). This section of the book is not looking at that
area: it is about helping students improve their *skills of listening*. Of course, neither
area is completely separate from the other; we need to know important vocabulary
and grammar in order to listen effectively. Having said that, it is still possible to see a
clear division of objectives between a lesson mainly aimed at working on language
systems and one aimed at working on language skills.

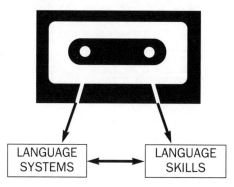

LANGUAGE SYSTEMS ←→ LANGUAGE SKILLS

On this cassette tape there is a two-minute recording of a scene in a wine bar.
Although it has been specially recorded for students of English, it sounds reasonably
authentic – ie it sounds spontaneous rather than scripted; the people are speaking at
normal speed and are not making unnatural efforts to enunciate or exaggerate stress
and intonation. We hear a couple briefly discussing the menu, then ordering two
meals and some wine. The waitress explains that one dish is 'off' so the man re-orders.
Here is a transcript of the tape.

MAN: Don't think I want meat today.
WOMAN: There's scampi ...
MAN: Can't stand it.
WOMAN: Could you just move the ... thanks.
MAN: Fresh caught cod – sounds good.
WOMAN: Should be at £7.95! Beef and stout pie – yuk! Mm lasagne – d'you think
              that's meat?
MAN: You're not vegetarian, are you?

WOMAN:	No, not really. Sort of 50/50. Excuse me.
	Is the lasagne vegetarian?
WAITRESS:	We do a vegetable one.
WOMAN:	Can I have that, please?
MAN:	And a cod and chips.
WAITRESS:	Sorry. The cod's finished. We do have scampi left.
MAN:	Oh – well – I'll have the same as her.
WAITRESS:	Right – anything to drink with the meal?
MAN:	I'll stick to wine, I think.
WOMAN:	I'll join you.
MAN:	A bottle of house red, please.
WAITRESS:	Thank you.

Task 1

Here is the opening of a lesson procedure intended to help improve students' listening skills:

Say to students: *Listen to this*. Play tape once. When finished, quickly ask individual students the following questions: **1** What price was the cod? **2** What was in the pie? **3** Why does the man choose lasagne? **4** What words did the man use to order the drink? Look coldly at students who get the answers wrong and tell them that they should have listened harder.

Apart from the insults, in what other ways might this lesson plan be unsatisfactory?

Commentary ■ ■ ■

This lesson is a parody of some language lessons that I was on the receiving end of as a student in school. I remember feeling quite nervous about them.

While I was listening I knew that some comprehension questions were going to come at the end, but I never knew what the questions might be or who would be asked to answer them. The questions, anyway, seemed pointless; they were not necessarily what I would listen for if I heard the conversation in real life – it was as if the teacher was focusing me on the difficulties rather than showing me that it was possible to achieve a lot *despite* the difficulties. The questions seemed more of a memory test than anything else. When the tape was played I struggled to listen to everything, and to remember all I heard, and in consequence actually remembered very little.

In fact, it's actually not necessary to understand every word in order to understand the information you might need from a recording. We need to show students this important fact – help them to worry less about understanding everything and work more on catching the bits they do need to hear.

There is really nothing in this lesson plan to help a student learn to listen better; either he can already listen and remember the required answers – or he cannot. But if he wants to improve his listening then he needs a different approach. ■

Task 2

Here is a second version of the same lesson plan:

Hand out a copy of the text of the conversation to all students. Play tape. When finished, ask individual students the following questions: **1** What does the man order? **2** What does the woman order?

There still seems to be a serious problem with this. What?

Commentary ■ ■ ■

The questions are a lot more sensible. The general tone is certainly less threatening! But the problem now is that the students don't actually need to listen at all. Giving out the text turns it into a reading exercise. Reading is usually easier for most students than deciphering the stream of speech and probably most students will work out the answers from the printed page rather than by struggling to listen.

If I sum up my feelings about Tasks 1 and 2, I get a checklist like this:

1 The activity must *really* demand listening.
2 It mustn't be simply a memory test.
3 Tasks should be realistic or useful in some way.
4 The activity must actively help them to *improve* their listening.
5 It shouldn't be threatening.
6 Help students work around difficulties to achieve specific results.

One way to achieve these goals is simple enough. By setting the questions *before* the tape is listened to (rather than after) we will give our students the opportunity to listen with a clear aim in mind. In everyday life we usually have some purpose in mind when we listen: to find out today's weather, to learn something, to be entertained, to discover what John did next, etc. By giving the learners a clear purpose in listening we turn the exercise from a memory test into a listening task. ■

Task 3

Look again at the lesson procedure in Task 2. Redesign it to take the checklist above into account.

Commentary ■ ■ ■

A simple plan would be as follows:

1 Set questions.
2 Play tape.
3 Check if the students have found the answers.
4 If not, go back to 2 as often as necessary.

This 'question first' technique is often characterized as 'task before tape'. The word 'task' reminds us that the activity the students are asked to do may be something more useful, more realistic, more motivating than simply finding answers to comprehension questions. ■

Task 4

Think of a task (other than finding answers to comprehension questions) to set students before listening to the restaurant scene on p 146.

Commentary ■ ■ ■

Some ideas:

• From a selection of pictures of food in the book, students pick out the items actually chosen by the couple.
• Students use a copy of the menu to calculate the bill the couple will have.
• The waitress is new and has made a lot of mistakes. Students correct mistakes on a copy of her notepad (eg beef lasagne).
• Students have a copy of the dialogue but with sentences in the wrong order; they must listen and arrange them in the correct order. ■

2   Task-based listening: some techniques

Some listening tasks are obviously more difficult than others. An important point (and typically a difficult one for newer teachers to come to terms with) is that the students getting the right answer is not necessarily the most important thing! A student who finds all the correct answers on first hearing and with no difficulty has simply not been challenged by the tape. It reflects over-simple tasks and little progress in listening has been made.

The effort that another student puts into listening and searching for an answer that is not easily found is, however, very useful work. Whether she finally gets the right or wrong answer is to some degree irrelevant, because in trying to get the right answer she is stretching her powers of listening to the limit. For this reason she will probably need to hear the tape played three, four or more times in order to get close to the target. Thus, the guideline 'process – rather than product' – meaning that the going is more important than the getting there. I'm not saying that getting wrong answers is good! But I am trying to steer you away from thinking that right answers are the only goal. The goal is the listening itself.

To help students listen better in this kind of lesson we may use some of the following techniques:

- Keep the recording short – not more than two minutes or so.
- Play the tape a sufficient number of times. (This is one point that teacher trainers and supervisors often comment on when they observe teachers' lessons: the teachers did not give the students enough opportunities to hear the tape. The students found the material a lot more difficult than the teacher realized.)
- Let students discuss their answers together (perhaps in pairs).
- Don't immediately acknowledge correct answers with words or facial expressions – throw the answers back to the class: *What do you think of X's answer – do you agree?*
- Don't be led by one strong student. Have they all got it?
- Aim to get the students to agree together without your help. Until they agree, play the tape again whenever they need to hear it, to confirm or refute their ideas.
- Play little bits of the tape (a word; a phrase; a sentence) again and again until it's clear.
- Give help if they are completely stuck – but still with the aim of getting them to work it out if at all possible (eg *There are three words in this sentence* or *Listen to what she says here*) rather than giving them the answers.
- Give them control of the tape recorder – to listen as and when and to what they wish.
- Don't cheat them by changing your requirements halfway – ie don't set one task but then afterwards ask for answers to something completely different!
- Don't let them lose heart. Try to make sure the task is just within their abilities. It should be difficult, but achievable. The sense of achievement in finishing a task should be great: 'It was difficult – but we did it!'

The last technique above leads us to another guideline: 'Grade the task – not the tape.' This means *Don't worry too much about what student level the recording is suitable for – but do make sure your task is set for the right level.* In theory it is possible to use any tape with any level – for example a recording of this morning's radio news. At beginner level I could ask them to catch the names of every famous person they heard. This could be challenging and stimulating. For a beginner to feel they have got something out of an authentic news tape! At a much higher level I could expect them to be able to understand most of the tape and do a sophisticated task like picking out unstressed words. In both cases it is *not* my material – the recording – that sets the level of the lesson: it is the task.

In practice, of course, some tapes are naturally going to seem more appropriate for specific levels of student. Thus a tape of someone asking for directions in the street is more likely to be usable at a lower level than, say, a discussion on complex moral issues.

Many teachers use a grading of tasks as a route-map through a listening lesson (see the diagram below). By starting with a simple task, letting them do it successfully, then moving on to set a more difficult task on the same tape, etc, the teacher can virtually let the class find its own level: ie you stop setting new tasks when you find the point at which they are beginning to struggle.

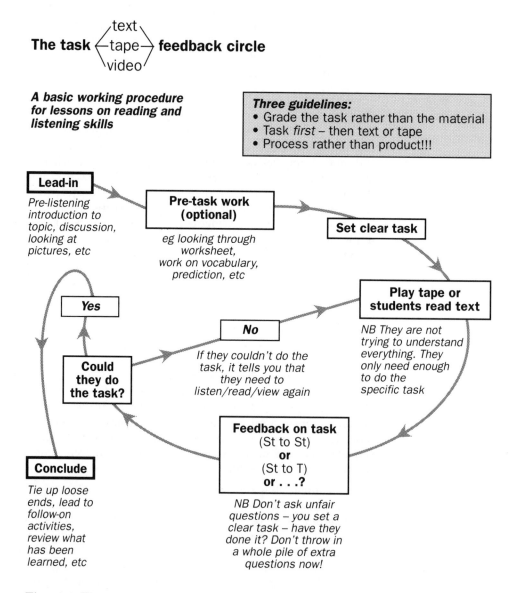

Fig. 10.1: The task–feedback circle

Commentary ■ ■ ■

One idea for a task: *You need to get your TV repaired. Find a useful phone number.*

Similar tasks might be *You're feeling very stressed! Who can help you?* or *Your computer has stopped working. Who can you call?* All these tasks involve students reading quickly and looking for specific items of information. They are also reading the material in the way one would do in everyday life. ■

Many activities designed to increase reading speeds are variations on the following two ideas:

- Read quickly and get the gist of a passage.
- Read quickly and find a specific piece of information.

The first of these ideas is also known as *skimming*. A typical skimming task would be a general question from the teacher such as *Is this passage about restaurants, offices or schools?* or *Why are these people at a meeting?* The learners would attempt to find the answer quickly, without reading every word of the passage, by 'speed-reading' through some portions of the text. Skimming is mainly concerned with finding key topics, main ideas, overall theme, basic structure, etc.

The second of the ideas is known as *scanning*. A common activity is searching for information in a leaflet or directory and a typical scanning task would be *What time does the Birmingham train leave?* or *Can I take my dog to Arundel castle?* or *What does Cathy take with her to the meeting?* Learners move their eyes quickly over the page, searching for key words or clues from the textual layout that will enable them to focus in on small sections of the text that they are likely to get answers from.

Task 3

Which of the following seem to be useful reading activities and which not? Why? Briefly work out an alternative procedure for the less satisfactory ones.

a The class reads a whole page of classified advertisements in the newspaper, using their dictionaries to check up all unknown words.
b The students each have a copy of *The Times* newspaper. The teacher asks them to find the word 'over' somewhere on the front page.
c The teacher throws a whole pile of tourist leaflets on the floor and explains that the students, in groups of four, can plan a day out tomorrow.
d The students read a short extract from a novel and answer five multiple choice comprehension questions about fine points of detail underneath.

Commentary ■ ■ ■

Procedure **a** seems unsatisfactory because it is an unrealistic use of the advertisements; in real life no one would read them in such a way. A more realistic task would require them to scan the ads for specific items (as we do when we want, say, to buy a second-hand TV). So: *What is the best TV I could buy?* would be a far more realistic task.

Procedure **b** is similarly strange. There is a scanning exercise – but an entirely unrealistic one. We might well scan the front page of *The Times* looking for names of people or countries that we wanted to read about – or headings that directed us to information we needed (such as weather). But it seems unlikely that we would search for a single word like *over* (though as a game, it could be fun). For a more useful scanning task students could be asked to find where specific articles are or find certain factual information. Skimming tasks would also be useful – to get the gist of an article.

Viewing

« Task-based listening: some techniques p 149

As with audio tapes, it usually helps to set clear viewing tasks and to follow similar procedures to those outlined in Chapter 10 Section 2 on listening. The task–tape–feedback circle still works well as a basic procedure for video. Tasks might be in the form of oral instructions or in the form of a worksheet, or they might be a natural follow-on from the preview activities. You may want to play the tape through many times with harder and harder tasks.

Tasks can be listening, looking, or interpreting. For example, *Why are they so keen to get into the museum after it's closed?* or *What seven things does the man do after leaving the gondola?* or *How does the shop assistant feel?* They can focus specifically on function, grammar, vocabulary or pronunciation. For example, *How many ways do the couple ask for help? Which of the following verbs does he use? What is on the shelf? Is she being polite or rude?* The answers to many of these questions will involve interpretation of the visual as well as the audio messages. Focusing on gestures, facial expressions, body language, etc is especially useful when studying functional language.

Follow-up

- discussion, interpretation, personalization (eg *What would you have done?* or *Has this ever happened to you?*);
- study of new language;
- roleplay the scene (or its continuation);
- inspiration for other work: *What did the newspaper/ Hello magazine say the next day? Design the front page*;
- write a letter from one character to another;
- plan what they should do next.

Exploiting video material

Those are the basics. Now, if you're feeling keen, here's a collection of ideas to liven up the lessons. (Don't try all of these in one go! But do try one or two of them sometime.)

- Don't let them mentally switch off – make them think; challenge them. Plan: cover up the screen: *Listen to the words/music – what's the picture? What are they describing? Where are they?* Then, when finished, look at the images and compare.
  In pairs, this becomes an instant communicative activity: *Tell your partner what you think was happening.* It could lead to drawing and comparison of pictures.
- Switch off the sound: *What are they saying?* Advertisements work beautifully: *In pairs, imagine and write the script.* And then the two students 'lip-synch' it: *Come up to the TV; sit on either side of it and while I play the (silent) tape again you speak the words.* (Hilarious – try it!)
- The stop button, pause button, freeze frame: *What happens next?* (Talk about it; write the story, etc.) Then (later) watch and compare.
- Divide the class in two, on separate sides of the room. Only one half can see the screen. Sound turned *off*. Half (A) watches for one minute. Then (as a group or in pairs) tells the other half (B) what happened. Then swap over and repeat. Great with short silent comedy sketches. For a very noisy variation: everyone in half A tells a pre-chosen partner in half B what is happening *while* it is happening – ie live commentary. The quiet variation: half A watches and *mimes* to half B what is happening; at the end half B must tell the story to half A. All of this sounds quite silly, but there's a lot of excellent speaking and listening practice.

- With a camera: make your own news/entertainment/documentary/advertisements.
- Film them doing something else and play back later for focus on pronunciation, grammar, effective communication, error analysis, etc.

Task 2

Recall a specific TV advertisement that you know well. Devise separate activities to use this in class to give students (a) speaking practice using past verb forms; (b) practice in writing formal letters; (c) a roleplay that does more than simply getting them to re-enact the ad.

Task 3

Find several ways to exploit a TV weather forecast in your class.

The final frame

I know quite a few teachers who never use video, even though their school has one available. It's true the machines (not to mention their cables) are often a real headache to set up and use and definite proof of the fact that 'They are against us.' But it's still worth persevering; I've found that if you (a) take a little time before the lesson to set it all up and (b) go in expecting the worst, the machines usually give in and let you have a useful and exciting lesson. It *will* all go wrong sometimes; the secret is simply not to panic when it does. The real key to a successful video lesson is always to have an emergency non-video lesson up your sleeve.

8   Testing

Your director of studies or head teacher has asked you to prepare a test for your class. How do you go about this?

You could test:

- the students' progress over the course so far (a progress test); or
- their general level of English, without reference to any course (a proficiency test).

Most internal school tests tend to be progress tests; most external ones (eg state or international exams) are usually proficiency tests.

‹‹ The subject matter of English language teaching p 20 When preparing progress tests you can test anything that has been studied; this usually means the four language systems and the four language skills. Remember your students' course has probably included not only reading and writing, grammar and vocabulary, but also speaking, listening, phonology and function. Somehow tests often seem to focus far more on the first four than the last four.

There are broadly speaking two kinds of ways to write the questions:

- discrete item questions (ie testing specific individual language points);
- integrative questions (ie a number of items or skills may be tested in the same question).

These can be marked in two ways:

- objectively (ie there is a clear correct answer and every marker would give the same marks to the same question);
- subjectively (ie the marking depends largely on the personal decision of the marker; different markers might give different marks for the same question).

Discrete items are likely to be marked objectively; integrative tests are more likely to be marked subjectively. Some questions may involve elements of both. Language systems are easier to test objectively; language skills tend to be tested subjectively.

A good test:

- will seem fair and appropriate to the students (and to anyone who needs to know the results – eg head teacher, other teachers, employers, parents, etc);
- will not be too troublesome to mark;
- will provide clear results that serve the purpose for which it was set.

Task 1

Decide if the following examples fulfil the three criteria for a good test given above.

a It is the day when new students arrive at your school. When you chat to them they seem to be very different in level. You give them a placement test to decide which level class they should go into. Everyone gets a mark between 63 and 67 out of 100.

b You set a test for your class using material from the next three units of the book that they will be studying over the next month.

c Your students have been studying a balanced course of skills and language improvement work for the last ten weeks. For the end of term test you have asked each student to write you five essays. It is now midnight and you have the pile of essays in front of you.

Commentary ■ ■ ■

(**a**) A test like this is virtually useless. A placement test needs to give a broad range of marks (eg between 10 and 90 out of 100) so that you can easily see who is stronger and who weaker.

(**b**) Do your class *know* why they are doing the test? You may have a very good reason for doing it, but if they don't know what that is, then it's going to seem a very unfair trick to test them on work they haven't done. However, if they *are* informed, then setting a test in advance like this could be very useful as a diagnostic tool to help you plan the course and allow them and you to see what they already know and what they need to work on. It would probably also be a good idea to do exactly the same test again at the end of the next part of the course in order to see (and let them see) what improvement they have made.

(**c**) Not really what you want to plough through late at night! It doesn't sound as if it fulfils the 'markability' criteria. Obviously there are going to be many occasions when it is essential to mark a great deal of written work, but there is no sense in creating unnecessary drudgery for yourself. This test hardly seems fair to students either; nor does it serve its purpose if it's intended to check on their progress (how can you measure progress in speaking, listening and reading with a purely written exam?). ■

Task 2

Categorize the following questions. Are they discrete? Integrative? Will the marking be objective or subjective? (The answer may not always be clear cut!)

1 Talk about this picture with your teacher. (Students are given a picture of people doing various things.)

2 Choose the word or phrase which best completes each sentence.
John always .... to the cinema on Saturday.
A go   B goes   C going   D gone

3 (In the language laboratory)
Voice on tape: 'Reply to these comments in a natural way.'
'Excuse me. Do you know where the nearest bus stop is?'
(10 second PAUSE)
'Would mind lending me your car, just for tonight?'
(10 second PAUSE)
'I've lost my watch. You don't have the time on you, do you?'
(10 second PAUSE)

4 Fill in the gaps:
a Have you .... been to Moscow?
b How long have you .... that new car?

5 You want to sell a new Walkman that you were given for Christmas (you already have one). Write a short notice to put on your school noticeboard.

6 (In a private interview with a teacher)
Read this aloud:
'The advertisement states that the new design measures 20 m x 35 m. If you are interested in receiving more information please contact Ms H.J. Jones of PORTILLO Warehouses, that's P - O - R - T - I - L - L - O Warehouses, on 071 489 2222 ext. 97.'

Commentary ■ ■ ■

Questions 2 and 4 seem to be clearly testing discrete items and to be suitable for objective marking, but even with simple examples such as Question 4, the matter is not quite so clear-cut. At first, it seems obvious. The answer to **4a** is *ever*. The answer to **4b** is *had*. But what about the student who writes *never* for **a** and *owned* for **b**? Both answers are perfectly good English. Do we have to write a marking scheme for **b** that includes *driven, wanted, desired,* etc? Or do we give a sample answer and leave it to the (subjective) discretion of the marker? Or do we give a mark only to the most obvious answer?

Another problem: what about the student who writes *been hoping to buy* for **b**? This is a problem with the instructions; although the small answer space allowed on the question paper *implies* 'one word' there is no instruction to that effect. Moral: make your instructions as complete and clear as possible.

The dividing line between subjective and objective is usually in the marking scheme. Question 6 could be marked by giving a subjective overall impression mark or it could be marked more objectively on discrete points (eg pronunciation of 20 m x 35 m – one mark for pronouncing numbers correctly, one mark for *by*; stress on *advertisement* = one mark; etc). ■

Some common discrete item testing techniques

Gap-fill

- **Single sentence**
  Fill in the blanks. Use only **one** word in each space.
  I'd .... go to the cafe than the pub.
  Answer: rather
  (If answers of more than one word are allowed then other answers are possible; instructions need to be clear!)

- **Cloze**
  A cloze test is a gap-fill exercise using a longer text and with a consistent number of words between gaps (eg every ninth word). The word 'cloze' is often incorrectly used to describe any gap-filling task.

- **Multiple choice**
  Choose the word or phrase which best completes each sentence.
  If I went to Jakarta .... buy some jewellery.
  a I'll   **b** I   **c** I will   **d** I'd
  Answer: **d**

- **Using given words**
  Put one word from the list below in each gap.
  He .... home late that night. As he .... the front door he .... he heard a noise in the sitting room. He tiptoed carefully into the room and .... on the light.

      thought   switched   unlocked   arrived

- **Using other clues** (eg pictures, lines indicating how many letters in word, etc)
  He looked through the _ _ _ _ _ _ and was amazed to see that she had finally come _ _ _ _ . (Students have pictures of a window and a house.)
  Answer: window; home

- **Transformation of a given word**
  He could produce no .... evidence to support his argument. (photograph)
  Answer: photographic

Sentence transformation

- **Starting with (or making use of) a given word or words; changing the form, but keeping the meaning**
  He liked the theatre but hated the play. (Although ...)
  Answer: Although he liked the theatre, he hated the play.

- **Following a given instruction**
  Change this sentence so that it describes the <u>past</u>:
  She's looking closely at the sculpture, trying to decide if she likes it.
  Possible answer: She looked closely at the sculpture, trying to decide if she liked it.

Sentence construction and reconstruction

- **Rearranging words**
  brother/much/he's/than/his/taller
  Answer: He's much taller than his brother.

- **Using some given words**
  Although/I/bad headache/go/concert
  Possible answer: Although I have a bad headache, I'll still go to the concert.

- **Finding and correcting mistakes**
  1 Cross out the incorrect word:
    When I will visit you I'll see your new baby.
    Answer: When I ~~will~~ visit you I'll see your new baby.
  2 Rewrite this sentence in correct English:
    I am enjoy swimming at the swimming pool of the sports centre.
    Possible answer: I enjoy swimming in the sports centre swimming pool.

- **Situational**
  You want to borrow some money from a colleague. What question would you ask?
  I wonder .... borrow .... ?
  Possible answer: I wonder if I could borrow ten dollars?

Two-option answers

- **True/false**
  (Often used after a reading passage eg *Paul wanted to visit the castle.* True/false?)

- **Correct/incorrect**
  Write [✔] if the following sentence is in correct English. If it is incorrect put a [✗].
  They always play football on Sundays.
  Answer: [✔]

- **Defined options**
  Jill is a fifteen-year-old schoolgirl. Mary is a one-year-old baby. Write **J** next to the things that belong to Jill. Write **M** next to the things that belong to Mary. (List: calculator; baby's bottle; teddy; Walkman; maths books.)

Matching (pictures, words, sentence pieces, labels, etc)

- **Pictures and words**
  Write the correct word under each picture.
  (sketches of transport)
  car bike ship motorbike van lorry caravan plane

- **Placing words in correct sets, lists, etc**

Food	Drinks	Meals
potatoes	milk	breakfast
rice	tea	dinner

  Put the following words in the correct list: water, cheese, wine, lemonade, lunch, bread, butter, supper

- **Grammatical labelling**
  Mark each sentence **a**, **b** or **c** depending on the tense used.
  a = present perfect; **b** = past simple; **c** = present continuous
  1 He's just come back.
  2 I've never been to the Andes.
  3 When did you go there?
  4 I'm living in Vienna at the moment.
  Answers: **1a 2a 3b 4c**

- **Putting jigsaw pieces together**
  Which beginning goes with which ending?

1	He planted	a	the stones and weeds
2	She picked	b	some beautiful red apples
3	She dug up	c	the seeds in three separate rows

  Probable answers: **1c 2b 3a**
  Note that some other answers are linguistically *possible* (eg **3b**), though they make less sense or seem more unlikely.

Task 3

Design three discrete item questions and one integrative question to test your understanding of this section of the book.

9   Exam classes

Many teachers at some point need to teach a class preparing for an exam. This may be a national or school exam or it might be one of the British or US-based international exams.

Fig. 11.10 shows the popular exams run by the Oxford and Cambridge Boards and their approximate level.

	Cambridge (UCLES)	Oxford	Oxford (ARELS)
Advanced	Proficiency (CPE)		Diploma
Post intermediate	Advanced (CAE)	Higher Certificate	Higher Certificate
Upper intermediate	First Certificate (FCE)		
Mid intermediate	Preliminary English Test (PET)	Preliminary Certificate	Preliminary Certificate
Low intermediate	Key English Test (KET)		
Elementary			
Beginner			
English language exams from Cambridge and Oxford: an approximate guide to comparative levels.			

Fig. 11.10: Oxford and Cambridge exams

A popular American English exam is TOEFL, which is geared towards testing English level prior to entering an American university. Of all these exams it is Cambridge First Certificate which seems to have established itself as the most widely accepted basic qualification in English and the exam is taken by a large number of students worldwide each year. Many students follow a preparation course before doing the exam. This section will concentrate on ways of planning for and teaching classes preparing for this or other exams.

An examination preparation course should probably include:

- language work that is likely to be relevant to that needed in the exam;
- tasks and activities to raise general language awareness, ability and skills;
- specific practice on exam techniques (eg multiple choice questions, writing essays, etc);
- work on study skills (eg use of dictionaries and grammar books, ways of working with tapes at home, etc).

Even if the exam is only concerned with reading and writing, there is still a strong case to be made for including a fair amount of speaking and listening work in the course, as the students' English is most likely to improve from balanced work on all skill areas as well as on grammar and vocabulary. It is also worth taking the time to help students learn some basic techniques for studying. A student who can understand the phonemic symbols in a dictionary, or who can take a tape home and use it efficiently, or who can make usable notes from the lessons, is likely to get more from the course than one who has not thought about these things. A basic skill that often needs some time assigned to it is how to organize your file/exercise book – do you just record page after page, day after day or do you try to organize it into sections at the start of the course (eg vocabulary, grammar, pronunciation, etc?).

« Remembering words p 88

A common problem with exam preparation courses arises when too much time is spent on exam technique and not enough on the other areas.

Teachers often feel pressure from students to do exam practice work, right from the start of a course, as if writing out countless mock tests will markedly improve their English. Clearly, students need to be very familiar with the form the exam takes, but doing practice tests alone will not in itself help the students to learn very much and can easily lead to 'burn-out'.

A more balanced approach for, say, a twelve-week course, might be to give students a lot of general language work and study skills in weeks one and two to give them the foundations for working successfully through the course. As the course progresses the study skills work could be reduced and much more specific work on typical language problems could be done. Work on examination technique would be introduced gradually and increasingly through the course and build up towards complete 'mock' tests in the week or two just before the exam.

It is often a good idea on exam preparation courses to be even more systematic than usual about what has been studied and to take care that items, once met, are recycled usefully. I have seen the following ideas used by a number of teachers on exam courses:

- **Posters**. When new language is studied, the students (or teacher) make posters to help them remember it. As the course progresses these slowly take over the room, acting as a very useful aide-memoire and a source of further work. I often find students browsing through these before class starts or in lunch breaks. Typical posters might be on phrasal verbs, tense problems, articles, present participle or infinitive? etc.
- **Vocabulary box/file**. Whereas posters are a good way of recording vocabulary, the sheer quantity of new words met on a course could soon fill the walls. An alternative is the 'vocabulary box'. At the end of each lesson (or day) the students review what they have learned that day, record any words worth recording on squares of paper (or card) and file them in the box or file. This is a good source of material for the teacher to exploit in future lessons (eg exercises and games recycling these words) and for students to look through.

Both of these ideas are of course also applicable to a wide variety of non-examination courses.

Finally, here are a few ideas to make practice of exam techniques a little more interesting. Many of these ideas also perform the essential task of raising awareness about how the tests are marked and the criteria the examiner will use.

- Students do exercises in pairs or small groups. (Possible rule: they MUST all agree on the same answer within each group.)
- Students mark each other's tests.
- 'Blitz' it: do an exercise at great speed – 10–20 per cent of the normal time allowance no thinking time – just do it! (Keep the atmosphere humorous – it's not a serious test.) *Then* let them go over it and consider their answers at leisure.
- A 'teacherless' lesson: give the students the chalk or board pens and they discuss and work through an exam paper together on the board. The teacher only looks at (and marks) the board when they have completely finished. (This is also a good 'group-building' exercise as it becomes a joint responsibility to get the best possible answers.)

- Students set tests in a particular style for each other (eg they take a text and rewrite it with gapped words; they prepare multiple choice questions on a text; etc).
- The teacher takes some written information about the exam (eg from a prospectus or a marking scheme) and turns it into exercises in the style of typical exam questions.
- The *teacher* does the exercise (including a mistake or two!) and the students correct it.

10 ESP and business English

ESP stands for English for Specific Purposes. That may mean English for hotel receptionists or English for pharmaceutical salesmen or English for telephoning. It may mean the rather wide-embracing title of 'business English'.

In one sense every individual student has his or her own 'specific purpose', even if it may seem a little vague in some cases – perhaps 'to improve my job prospects' or 'to make my holidays more interesting'. ESP contrasts with the rather mischievous acronym LENOR (Learning English for No Obvious Reason); it implies that we are going to take the client's needs and goals more seriously when planning the course and rather than teach 'general English' we are going to tailor everything to his or her character and particular requirements.

But I don't know about nuclear fission and I have to teach a three-week ESP course for nuclear engineers ....! Don't panic! You are an English teacher; no one expects you to know anything about nuclear power (other than what the person-in-the-street might know). *You* know about English; *they* know about the topic. Put the two together and you have the potential for some exciting lessons. For one thing, there is a genuine information gap and thus a real reason for communication. The learners can speak and write about their field of work and do appropriate tasks that they need to perform in English. You can help them find ways to do this more effectively.

Thus ESP really means: *Go on teaching all the normal English you already teach in all the ways you know how to do already but use vocabulary, examples, topics and contexts that are, as far as possible, relevant to the students and practise relevant specific skills. If you don't have the appropriate texts/tapes/etc to hand then it may be possible to get your students to provide them.*

A good starting point for ESP teaching is a 'needs analysis' or a 'client map'. We can't teach a student's specific needs unless we are absolutely clear about what they are. A typical needs analysis might be a questionnaire that the client(s) and teacher talk through and fill in together. This might include an analysis of what the client uses English for, what their expectations are, what they need, what they want and what they don't have.

One point to bear in mind is that ESP courses are sometimes booked and paid for by people other than those who actually do them (eg a company training manager arranges for an executive to study on an intensive two-week course). Sometimes the wants of the two may be very different and the teacher may find it a hard act to balance.

Task 1

For each of the following specific skill requirements, find one activity that you could do in the classroom to practise it.

a Travel agent: taking telephone bookings for flights
b R & D manager: making presentation to large conference audience about new products
c Marketing manager: sending short, clear fax messages to overseas representatives
d Company director: meeting important clients on social occasions
e Hotel receptionist: dealing with foreign holidaymakers

Commentary ■ ■ ■

The following activities are some possibilities:

a Design an information gap activity that involves one person knowing names, numbers, etc that they have to communicate to the other person so that they can write it down.

```
Book flight to Athens on
13th Feb in the morning
if possible
Pete Martineau
```

```
Flights to Athens leave
at 02.45, 09.05, 12.35,
17.55.
Book flight for . . . . .
on . . . . . at . . . . . .
```

The activity could be done in pairs in class or between teacher and learner in a one-to-one lesson.

b Find a detailed description of a product in a magazine. Give the article to the learner to (1) read for homework, (2) discuss and study in class, (3) prepare a presentation to give to the other students and/or the teacher.

c Set aside one section of the lesson in which to communicate only by writing. The students sit in separate parts of the room. Give each person a pile of blank 'fax' paper and get writing. The students only approach other people in order to deliver messages they have written. This activity works well simply on a personal 'letter-writing' level, but if each person involved also has some specific information to hand, or has some specific tasks to achieve (eg *Find out who is offering the lowest price for a transport contract and agree a deal with them*) then the activity can be very demanding and useful.

d Roleplay an appropriate meeting and (either before or after) study the language that seemed most useful. Video the activity for more detailed analysis.

e The receptionist 'real-plays' himself/herself while other students and/or the teacher roleplay a variety of guests. (Again, video recording would be useful.) ■

11 Learner training

For me, learner training means *Raise student awareness about how they are learning and, as a result, help them to find more effective ways of working, so that they can continue working efficiently and usefully even when away from their teacher and the classroom.* More simply, it means *work on teaching **learning** as well as teaching English.*

Learner training, therefore, includes:

- work on study skills, eg use of dictionaries, reference material, workbooks, notebooks, filed material;
- student examination of the process of learning and reflection on what is happening.

In both cases, it seems important to include these as strands throughout a course.

Three ideas:

1 Integrate study skills work

Include study skills work as an integrated feature of your lessons – eg when working on vocabulary, include a short exercise that involves efficiently looking up information in a dictionary. Similarly, when the students have found some new words to learn, you could make them aware of the variety of ways of recording vocabulary in their notebooks.

« Remembering
words p 88

2 Let them into the secret

Teachers sometimes prefer the 'surprise' approach to teaching methodology; often students don't really know why they followed a particular procedure or did a particular activity. Teachers often assume that their own reasoning will be transparently obvious to their students, but it rarely is. So it can be very useful to tell students before a lesson what's going to happen and *why*. At the end of the lesson, you can review not only the content, but also the way that it was studied.

For example, after a listening skills lesson, talk through the procedure with the students: *Why did I set a task first? Was it necessary to understand every word? What did we do next? What helped you learn? What didn't help?*

In this way they will also be learning a methodology that they can repeat for their own use when they listen to a cassette at home or in a language laboratory.

3 Discuss process as well as content and procedure

The content of your lessons is the English language. The 'procedures' are your methodology (which I suggested above was worth talking about with students). The third area is 'process'. By this I mean the lesson as viewed from the learner's point of view. You're doing certain things as a teacher but what is going on for each individual student?

It can be very valuable to set aside time in class simply to discuss the subject of 'learning on this course' in order to recall what's happening and reflect on it. This 'process review' will allow teachers and learners to clarify what is happening. Simply talking about what is going on seems to have a very beneficial effect, quite apart from any new ideas or solutions that arise from it.

12 Dealing with constraints and problems

This section describes four common situations faced by EFL teachers the world over:

1 Your class is very large, with a range of abilities in it.
2 You want students to use English in class, but the students do most things in their own language.
3 The course requirements are unrealistic or unsuitable. For example, the only book you've got to use is awful but the students/head/syllabus/inspector require you to use it.
4 A student, or students, complain(s) about your lessons.

This section is divided into four parts, each dealing with one of these situations. In each case there is a suggested assessment procedure that may help you to analyze the problem and clarify your own solutions to the questions. Although these procedures are associated with the specific problem, they are designed to be applicable to a range of different difficulties.

Situation 1: Large classes

In many countries teachers find that the main constraint on creative teaching is the sheer size of their classes. Of course, 'large' is relative; it depends on what you are used to. If you are used to groups of eight students, then you might regard twenty-five as large. Some teachers regularly teach classes of forty students, others eighty. Some teachers work with a hundred or more students at a time.

Some common resulting difficulties:

- students can't move easily;
- the teacher can't move easily;
- the seating arrangement seems to prevent a number of activities;
- there is limited eye-contact from teacher to students;
- there is limited or no eye-contact amongst students;
- you can't give attention equally to all students;
- interaction tends to be restricted to those closest to the front;
- the seats at the back tend to attract people who want to do something other than learn English;
- people 'hide' away;
- there is often a very wide range of abilities;
- discipline can be a problem;
- lecturing seems to be the only workable lesson type;
- a lot of techniques outlined in this book seem impossible.

I hesitate to propose any easy solutions to such problems, mainly because I don't know about your specific situation and the particular constraints you have. I can offer you two things: (1) an assessment procedure that may help you towards finding your own solutions to your own problems; and (2) my own belief that there are probably many options available in response to any problem, and that, surprisingly, the constraining factor is often our own worry or doubts or our fear of trying something different from what is normally done.

Procedure 1: Working with constraints

a Define the problem

Write a brief definition of one specific problem that acts as a constraint on your teaching. For example: *I can't use groupwork and pairwork in my class because there are so many students and they can't move from their seats.*

b Analyze and rewrite the problem

Break the problem up into any smaller or component problems. For example, the sentence in (a) above seems to contain four separate components: *I can't use groupwork; I can't use pairwork; There are a lot of students;* and *They can't move from their seats.*

Now rewrite your definition of each component problem, trying to word the new descriptions as honestly as possible to show the true nature of the constraints – eg is it entirely a limit imposed from outside? Or is it a personal decision not to do something? Be specific about your own thoughts and fears. For example, in the fourth component part, I wrote *They can't move from their seats.* In the rewritten version I put *I choose not to get the students to move from their seats because I think it would be difficult, very noisy and I am frightened that there would be chaos in the room.*

c Brainstorming

Choose one of these component problems and make a list of all the possible, impossible, completely impossible and fantastic options that would help to solve this problem. Don't censor your brainstorming. Don't stop to question or think about what you are writing. Simply allow a two- or three-minute period when you turn on the tap and let your ideas flow out. Look for options within you as well as for things outside yourself.

For example: *rearrange the seating; move to a different class; get them to climb over the seats; push the seats up against the wall; get half the students to turn around and face the students behind them; let them sit on the desks; stand on the desks to do the activity; go into the school hall for English lessons; go outside on the grass; don't worry about the noise; take the risk that getting them to move will be OK; find out how other teachers do it; ask the students what they think about these ideas – what's their solution; negotiate a contract – quiet movement in exchange for more variety of activities.*

d Reflecting on options

When the flow of ideas seems to be coming to an end, go back slowly over the list and consider each one. Reflect on whether it is practicable, what might prevent it working, why you don't do it, how 'risky' it would be for you to try it out, etc.

e Action planning

Make a simple statement of what you intend to do – perhaps a small 'try-out' of one idea in your next class. Choose modest steps. For example: *Next lesson I will try a short five-minute speaking activity where I will ask the students to turn around and work with the student in the row behind them* or *I will talk with the deputy head teacher and find out if our class can use the school hall for the Tuesday afternoon class.*

Situation 2: Students using their own language

They always talk in their own language. I can't get them to use English.
This is a common problem in monolingual classes, especially with children and young adults. What might the reasons be?

- Because it's easier to speak my own language.
- Because the teacher always corrects me if I speak English.
- Because I don't want to get it wrong in front of others.
- Because it's not 'in' to speak in English.
- Because the teacher is only pretending not to understand my own language.
- I need to use my own language because I can't say what I want in English.
- Because it's silly to speak English. It's much easier to communicate in the language we all understand.
- Because ...

Using English in class

Some teachers have found that competition and bribery are techniques that get results (eg *Every time you speak Spanish I'll give a red mark to your team. The team with the least red marks at the end gets a bar of chocolate.*) I have some problems with this as it seems to be building a motivation quite separate from the genuine interest in the subject matter that I am hoping to arouse; it seems to be a case of *Do this to please the teacher.*

I am sure that inducements, threats, prizes, etc can all have a limited success in creating an 'English-only' classroom, but I believe that a more complete solution involves looking at the whole atmosphere of the class.

As an ideal, I would like a classroom where learners were free to use their own tongue whenever they wanted, but in fact mostly *chose* to use English. How would this be possible? Perhaps by creating a climate where it was OK to use English, where using English was normal and natural and not special or frightening. There is no easy way to get to this, but here are some ideas that might help:

- Use lots of listening material to surround them in the sound of English.
- Make the room 'English'.
- Have short, clearly demarcated sections of the lesson when English is the first language; at other times other languages are possible.
- Negotiate the ground rules with the students or, better, let them set them completely by themselves.
- Discuss (as opposed to *tell*) the point of the activity, lesson, course. Agree how it will be done, why using English is important.
- Respond positively to every effort at using English.
- Don't tell off learners for not using English but keep operating in English yourself.
- Only 'hear' English.
- Spend a lot of time on fluency work without correction.
- Establish that you are delighted for them to speak any English at all – communication is your priority, rather than accuracy.
- Create lots of pair and small group activities that require them to do something with English without the loss of face of getting it wrong in a bigger group.
- When it becomes a big problem, stop the activity, and negotiate again: *I notice that many of you are using Portuguese. Is this OK?*
- Be prepared for English use to grow gradually rather than be established for a whole lesson at the start of the course.

Procedure 2: Seeing things from a different viewpoint: changes

Imagine yourself as a specific individual student in your class. What change in the teacher, students, atmosphere, activities, lessons, etc would make you comfortable, or even keen, to ... use English in class?

(This task can easily be used for a variety of situations by changing the words after the dots.)

Situation 3: Unrealistic requirements

Teachers are often faced with syllabus requirements that they don't agree with or teaching material that they don't like. There is a fine balance between doing what you are required or expected to do and doing what you believe is appropriate, useful or needed.

There is obviously no single, magic answer to problems of this kind. However, it is often possible to do what is expected of you, to reach the goals you have been told to reach, to use the pages of the book you have been told to use, to get students through tests they need to pass, to make the end point of the lesson, the day, the course exactly where it is supposed to be, but still to make the journey there surprising, interesting and exciting. The parabola ends up at the same point, but follows a much more interesting route than the straight line.

Some examples:

- Your boss has told you that the only aim of your course is to get students to pass a (very boring) written grammar and essay exam at the end of term.

  The straight line approach is to spend all the class time doing grammar and written work. The parabola is to follow a balanced syllabus that includes a lot of speaking, listening and other skills work of all kinds as well as grammar and vocabulary. Sometimes the parabola is the shortest road; you may find that the students make much better progress and get better results than students who only follow the straight line.

- You have been told that you must 'do' two pages of the coursebook every day. The whole book must be covered by the end of the term.

  The straight line would be to work through everything in the coursebook as it is written, doing each exercise in order, in the way that the coursebook writer tells you to. The parabola is to use the two pages every day as required, but really exploiting them, using them as resource material. Change the order! Get students to cross out boring exercises! Design better pictures for a text! Debate with the students how to use the book! Agree with students to speed through six pages in one day (and free yourself for two days)! Supplement with lots of your own goodies! Turn texts into dictations, information gaps, listenings, games, etc!

Straight lines are boring. Be bold – travel by parabola.

Procedure 3: Defining radical alternatives

Choose one current difficulty or problem in your teaching. Define what the straight line and the parabola are for it.

Situation 4: Student complaints

Students do complain, sometimes at unexpected times, just when you think the course and the lessons are going really well. Sometimes it's one student who catches you in the corridor, sometimes a whole deputation at the end of a lesson. It can be a shock to realize that your own intuitive perception of their views is completely wrong.

Sometimes it can be more serious. Many teachers have been through an unnerving moment when a student or a class has gone to the Head and complained about them – that they're not doing this or doing too much of that, or they don't like the way they do this. It can feel very destructive; but (once the shock and immediate pain have passed) it can also be a real chance to move forward.

Procedure 4: Seeing things from a different viewpoint: participation

- Imagine yourself as one specific student in your own class. What would you say about your teacher, the lessons and the course if you had the chance?
- Have you been given a real chance to say this by your teacher? (ie not a quick *how are you* question but genuine, honestly intentioned opportunities to say what you want).
- If the answer to the last question is *no*, why do you think this is? How could it be different?
  If the answer is *yes*, has the teacher really listened and taken account of what you said or was the operation more cosmetic?
- As the teacher, how do you feel about this student?

Unexpected complaints usually come when the teacher has been unwilling or unable to allow the learners genuine chances to say what they want to. This sounds easy enough to do; in practice it can be quite difficult. Inexperienced teachers, in particular, may feel they have enough insecurities and doubts themselves without giving the students a chance to add to these. It's quite easy then to avoid the dialogue and simply to keep on going on. Or to create the illusion of a dialogue, but in fact to avoid the real questions, or to ask questions in such a way that the students know what is expected of them. Or to ask, but then not listen.

A suggestion: regularly allow some completely unstructured time to discuss things – where they are going, how they feel about it, etc. Use this time to listen; don't attempt to set the agenda too much, or to reply to everything; the more you justify and explain, the more likely the learners are to clam up.

Chapter 12 **Learning teaching**

1   Feedback and reflection

Teaching English can be very exciting, but at 3.30 on a Monday afternoon, with a whole term ahead of you, it can seem a lot of other things too.

For the first two years or so in the profession the demands of getting to grips with subject matter, technique, organization, school politics, not to mention students, can be very stressful and tiring and it may often feel as if you stand no chance at all of winning through. Ideals and enthusiasm that you started with may fade away as it becomes clear that you can't make every lesson perfect, that some students, some classes simply won't like what you do. And there are the days when you may have to struggle just to get through.

As time goes on you will probably find that you have more experience to lean on, more tried and tested lessons in the bag, to recycle endlessly. Then boredom and staleness are the dangers, once the challenge of becoming competent has faded. Twenty years of teaching experience can become no more than two years' experience repeated ten times over. Repeated venturing down well-travelled roads leads sooner or later to boredom, to fossilization of routines, to increasing defensiveness and fear of change. The question becomes not *How can I survive?* but *How can I keep moving forward?* or *How can I become the best teacher that I can be?* The more established and safer you are in your job, the harder it can become to take risks, to try something completely different.

The first important steps towards becoming a better teacher involve an *increased awareness about what I do now and an openness to the possibility of change.*

If I want to move forward I have to be clear about what it is that I do now. Do I actually *know* what I am doing in class? Do I ever stop and examine my actions, my intentions, my motives, my attitudes? I keep planning for the next lesson, the next day, but to look back, to recall what happened, to reflect on it – this seems harder to do. What *did* happen in that class? What was I like as a teacher? Did I enable learning or prevent it? Why did I do the things I did? What were the other options – the ones that I didn't take?

<< The experiential learning cycle p 3

We can teach and teach. Or we can teach and learn. This kind of teaching, a 'learning teaching', is a refusal to say 'I know it all. I can relax for the rest of my career.' Learning teaching is a desire to move forward, to keep learning from what happens. It involves feedback from others and from ourselves about what happened. It involves reflection on what happened, together with an excitement about trying a slightly different option next time. Learning teaching is an aware and active use of the experiential learning cycle in one's own life and work. Learning teaching is a belief that creativity, understanding, experience and character continue growing throughout one's life.

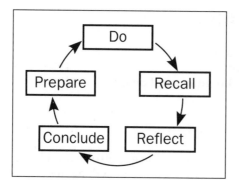

Feedback from learners

Don't be frightened of encouraging genuine feedback – it is avoiding feedback or ignoring it that often leads to the serious problems. Ask the learners in your class what they really think. If your intention is only to hear 'nice things', then that is probably all you will get – bland comments of no use to anyone. But set aside some time, ask open questions that enable them to say what they want to say and feel the intention within yourself simply to listen and learn (rather than to defend yourself, argue or to contradict). The feedback may be difficult for you the first time, but the end result of increased honesty, openness and mutual respect will almost certainly have a great long-term benefit, the more so if you implement changes in yourself, the class or the course that are responses to the feedback.

Feedback from others: colleagues

Ask other teachers to come in and observe some of your lessons, and do an exchange observation with them, not to judge each other or score points but to learn from each other. The growth in trust and respect that comes from sharing ideas and skills in this way can really help all involved move forward, as well as having a markedly positive effect on the whole atmosphere of a school.

Even if a colleague cannot come in and observe a lesson, then you could still set aside some uninterrupted time (perhaps fifteen minutes or so) when they will sit and listen to you talk through your thoughts about the lesson. Your colleague will make a 'contract' with you that he or she will not offer suggestions or advice or help or opinions, but will simply listen and support you. This kind of helping is very simple to describe but extremely powerful in action. It can be surprisingly beneficial to talk through one's own experience with another person who is really listening.

Feedback from you

When you have taught a lesson it can be tempting to see it completely uncritically in broad shades of extremes either as a huge success or as a complete failure. Teachers sometimes find themselves diving from one extreme to the other in the space of a few minutes.

You may equally be tempted not to think about the lesson at all – to put it away in the back of your mind and forget it, or alternatively to brood over it, picking away at it for hours afterwards, regretting what happened and seeing every possible alternative way of doing things as an improvement on what actually happened.

The alternative (and more difficult option) is to try and take an objective, more balanced view of what happened: first to recall what happened, then to reflect on that and look for what was successful and for what could be improved. Whatever the lesson was like, there will have been good points in it and things that could be worked on. This is true for the most experienced teacher as much as for a beginner.

If you are taking an initial training course then your tutors may be just as interested in encouraging your own self-awareness as in pointing out successes and problems themselves. They could spend the whole time praising what you did, or tearing your lesson into little pieces, but the only thing that is going to move you forward as a teacher is if you yourself become aware of what works and what doesn't.

'Two-stage feedback' is one way of becoming more aware of what you are doing. It works like this:

- As soon as you sit down after teaching (and as soon as you have got your breath back!) write down (a) a description of some of the things that happened, and/or (b) your first reactions and feelings about what happened. None of this needs to be more than a sentence or two; you may find that the simple act of trying to get your thoughts together in writing will help you to clarify exactly what it is that you are thinking. For example:

The oral practice seemed to work well. The students got really involved and didn't want to stop. I noticed that I was concentrating on students to my right; I rather left out the five sitting near the door. Checking the homework with the whole class was very dull. There must be a better way to go through all the answers.

- When the lesson has become a bit clearer in your head – maybe an hour or so later, or perhaps the next day (or, if the lesson was observed, after the observer has talked over the lesson with you) add a few more sentences, remembering to look for the positive things as well as things that need work. For example:

What was successful: the vocabulary game - fast and fun - they practised a lot of words. I felt more confident this lesson; I'm beginning to get used to the way this class works. To work on: I could be clearer with instructions. They were definitely confused at the start of the game. I talked rather a lot. I noticed myself talking over some of their answers when I got impatient - I'll try to watch for that in future. I don't think Joanna said anything all lesson. I must have a chat with her and find out if everything's OK. Perhaps I could ask questions direct to named individuals, rather than general questions to the whole class. That would stop the two strong ones always coming in first.

The 'feedback' sheet will now represent your views at two different stages of considering the lesson. You may well find that your reaction is rather different at these two points. Finding which view of these two is the most objective and realistic and supportive to yourself may improve your ability to analyze your own lessons in the future, and thus help your development as a teacher.

Your own approach to this kind of self-feedback will reflect your own style and your own perceptions, but if you find it hard to get going, try using the self-assessment model described on p 198.

Lesson self-assessment

For each lesson you teach, choose one question from part **A** below, one from part **B**, and one from part **C**. Write your answers. If possible, talk through your answers with another person who has agreed simply to *listen* (rather than take part in a conversation).

Roughly speaking, **A** focuses you on recalling what happened in the lesson. **B** focuses on reflecting on the lesson, particularly looking for what was successful. **C** focuses on drawing conclusions from the experience and finding ways to move forward in your future teaching.

A Recalling the lesson

1 List a number of things that you (the teacher) did during the lesson.
2 List a number of things that the learners did during the lesson.
3 Note down any comments or feedback that a student gave you during the lesson.
4 Note any important personal interaction between you and a student during the lesson.
5 Summarize the main stages of the lesson as you remember it.
6 What was the balance of 'teacher doing things' compared with 'students doing things' in the lesson?
7 List some things that happened approximately as you planned them.
8 List some things that happened differently from your plan.
9 Recall one moment in the lesson when you had a clear decision to make between one option and another. What were the options you chose and rejected?

B Reflecting on the lesson

1 Note several things that you are proud of about the lesson.
2 What was the high point of the lesson for you? Why did it feel good?
3 Can you answer that same question from the learners' point of view?
4 Name several specific points in the lesson where you feel the learners were learning something.
5 At what points could you have been clearer?
6 Which part of the lesson involved the learners most completely?
7 Where was time not used efficiently?
8 At what point did you feel most awkward or uncomfortable?
9 Did you achieve what you wanted to achieve?
10 Did the learners achieve what you hoped they would achieve?

C Drawing conclusions; making plans

1 If you taught the lesson again, what would you do the same?
2 If you taught the lesson again, what would you do differently?
3 What have you learned about your planning?
4 What have you learned about your teaching procedures and techniques?
5 What have you learned about your learners?
6 What have you learned about yourself?
7 What have you learned about learning?
8 List some intentions or 'action plans' for your future teaching.
9 Write a brief description of yourself as a teacher seen from a student's viewpoint. What is it like to be taught by you?

2   Teacher development

The dangers

Some ideas for moving forward

- Read new ideas in magazines and try them out
- Write an article for a magazine (most articles in magazines for language teachers are by teachers like you)
- Start a local teachers' newsletter
- Try a bold parabola
- Go to a conference or a seminar
- Learn about a completely different approach
- Join (or start) a teacher development group
- Discuss what you are doing with other teachers
- Make an agreement with a colleague to observe each other's lessons
- Find a way to get involved in some in-service teacher training
- Become a director of studies or a headteacher!
- Start your own school!
- Give private lessons
- Specialize (eg computers, business, self-access centres, video, music, exams, etc)
- Write a book. (This, as you will have noticed, is what I'm doing now; it's my own personal solution to moving myself forward at the moment.)